BASKETRY FOR EVERYONE

CAVENDISH HOUSE

Edited by Yvonne Deutch
Designed by Barbara Maynard

Published by Marshall Cavendish Books Limited
58 Old Compton Street, London W1V 5PA

© Marshall Cavendish Limited, 1976, 1983

First printing 1976 (softback)
Second printing 1983 (hardback)

Printed by L.E.G.O., Vicenza, Italy

ISBN 0 86307 064 7

Introducing basketry

Basketry is one of the oldest crafts and has lasted since the beginning of history, adapting itself to various needs throughout the centuries.

It was Britain's first export industry, and the only one when the Romans first arrived. The ancient Britons were extremely good at basketry and made such articles as farm carts and wagons in wicker work. Many of the terms used in basketry even today are of Anglo-Saxon origin.

Many different materials, from cane to willow, are used for basketry and each material has its own particular techniques and adaptations.

Materials

Cane comes from the rattan family which is a creeper from SE Asia. It grows to enormous lengths and has sharp barbs. The outer layer is peeled off and discarded, while the bark is used for chair seating and handle wrapping. The inside pith or pulp is milled into canes of many thicknesses, from 000 (1mm) to 16 (5mm), and handle cane of 8mm or 10mm.

There are various qualities (all natural coloured, of course), 'blue tie' being

Preparation

Cane must be soaked in hot water for about 30 minutes before using. Once you start you will soon be able to gauge the soaking time. If it dries while you are working just re-soak it until it is easy to handle.

When you stop allow the work, plus all remaining cane, to dry before you put it away. Do not put damp cane into plastic bags as it will go mouldy.

Tools

The tools and equipment needed are inexpensive and some can be home-made and some improvised.

Side cutters, obtainable from tool shops, are useful but strong scissors, such as those used for flower arranging, or even garden secateurs will do.

A basket maker's bodkin is essential. It is used to form channels for canes to thread into or to split the cane. You can buy one from a craft supplier or improvise with an old, sharpened screwdriver or a medium-sized knitting needle.

Tape measure.

Clothes pegs are useful for temporarily holding the work in place.

the best, 'red' or 'green tie' and finally 'white tie' or bleached cane, which is rather poor in quality. Seagrass, strawplait, raffia, enamelled cane or wrapping cane can all be used to add colour and interest; cane can also be dyed with fabric dye.

Tools and materials include cane, basket maker's bodkin, secateurs (top) and side cutters (bottom).

1

A picnic basket

Techniques

There are various ways to begin a basket. Initially you can use a plastic or wooden base with holes in it made specially for basket making. You can use any base to suit your requirements as long as it has an odd number of holes.

However, as these bases limit the design potential, only use them in order to become familiar with the materials. The holes in the base are not always big enough to hold thick cane which means that you cannot make a large, sturdy basket. Bases also tend to make a basket heavy. How-

ever, the picnic basket illustrated is useful and makes an introduction to the various terms.

The picnic basket

The strong basket overleaf will give you years of use. It is designed to hold two flasks and a sandwich box in the middle.

You will need:
227gm ($\frac{1}{2}$lb) No.8 (3mm) cane.
113gm ($\frac{1}{4}$lb) No.5 (2.5mm) cane.
3m (3yd) 10mm handle cane.
5.5m (6yd) glossy wrapping cane or 7.5m (8yd) No.6 (2.6mm) chair seating cane.

The baskets are made using a plywood or laminated plastic base. The larger one is ideal for picnics and the smaller one is a child's basket.
Designed by Barbara Maynard.

1m (1yd) enamelled cane—optional.
56gm (2oz) sea-grass—optional.
Oblong plywood or plastic base 15cm x 41cm (6″x16″) with 49 holes.

☐ Prepare the cane by soaking it in hot water for 30 minutes.

For the ribs, ie the upright stakes; cut 49 stakes of No.8 (3mm) cane 51cm (20″) long. Insert one stake into each hole allowing 10cm (4″) to protrude on the wrong side of the base. If the cane is difficult to push through the holes you can widen them with the bodkin. Alternatively, as the cane swells when wet, insert the canes before soaking and soak them afterwards.

To make a foot border under the basket.

☐ Hold the base with the right side towards you and the short stake ends away from you. Starting with any stake end, bend it down to the right behind the next stake and back to the front. Then pass it in front of the next 2 stakes and tuck it to the back through the next space (fig.1).

☐ Repeat with each stake in turn. It will help if you say to yourself "Behind one, in front of two, and tuck it in". At the end of the round weave the stakes in and out of stakes that have already been turned down. You may have to push these stakes up a bit to get the others through. When they are all in place, give each stake a little pull to see that they are all tight and level.

☐ Place the basket right side up on the table. Put some sort of weight (a stone, flat iron) inside the basket to keep it steady. This will make it easier to hold the work and also to keep the shape you want.

Now you have to wale. Waling is a weave used for strength and is put on the bottom and the top of a basket. When a basket starts to lose its shape, a band of waling will help to retain it. It can be done with 3, 4, 5 or 6 weavers —for this basket use 3 weavers.

☐ Insert 3 lengths of No.5 (2.5mm) cane, to be used as weavers, into any 3 consecutive spaces. Mark the stake immediately to the left of the first one in some way. Take the left hand weaver to the right in front of 2 stakes, over the top of the other 2 weavers and round the back of the next stake to the front again (fig.2).

☐ Now use the next left hand weaver and do exactly the same as before and then repeat with each weaver in turn all the way round the basket and back to the marked stake (fig.3).

Here you have to do a 'step-up'. If you don't, the work jumps up and spirals and the weave doesn't have the continuous rope effect that it should. You have to do this step-up at this spot on every round and then continue

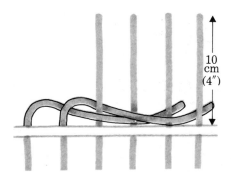

1. *The foot border.*

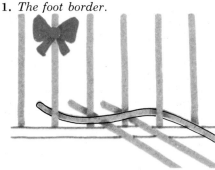

2. *The start of waling.*

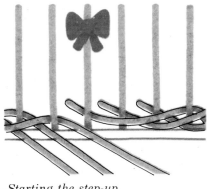

3. *Starting the step-up.*

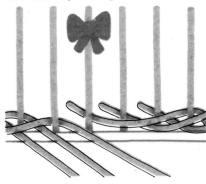

4. *First stage of step-up.*

5. *The step-up completed.*

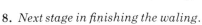

6. *Joining new cane in waling.*

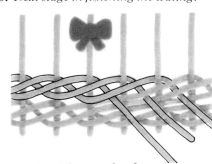

7. *The end of the waling.*

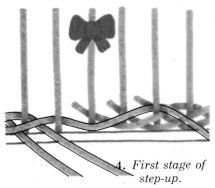

8. *Next stage in finishing the waling.*

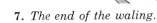

9. *The completed waling before trimming the ends.*

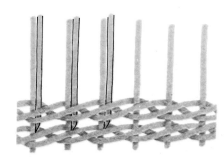

10. *Inserting bye-stakes.*

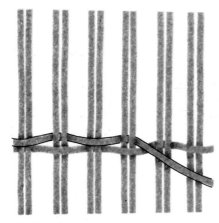

11. *Randing.*

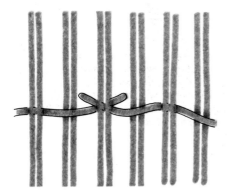

12a. *Front view of a new cane being joined in randing.*

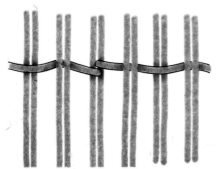

12b. *Back view of join with the ends trimmed back.*

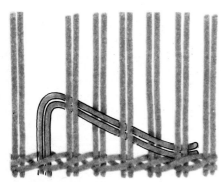

14. *Starting a trac border.*

as you started.

☐ Take the right hand weaver in front of 2, behind one and through to the front again (fig.4).

☐ Take the middle one in front of 2 and behind one. Take the left one in front of 2 and behind one (fig.5).

All the weavers should now come out of the same 3 spaces you started with.

☐ Continue until you reach the marked stake again and step-up.

☐ Put on 5 rounds of waling, remembering to step-up at the marked stake, joining in new lengths when necessary.

Joining weavers. Join in when the cane which has run out is on the left of the other weavers. Pull it backwards slightly and insert the new cane into the hole beside, and to the right of, the old one. This means that the old and new weavers will lie side by side and the old end will be to the front and the new end will be inside the basket (fig.6). The ends are tidied later.

☐ To complete the 5 rounds of waling use the left hand weaver (not the right one this time), in front of 2, behind one and to the front again. This will go round the back of the marked stake. Cut it off to about 7.5cm (3″) (fig.7).

☐ Now use the next left hand weaver and pass it in front of 2, behind one and through to the front, but on its way to the front thread it under the top cane of the previous round. Cut this one off (fig.8).

☐ Use the last weaver now, in front of 2 and behind one, but thread it under the top 2 canes of the previous round, and cut it off (fig.9).

Bye-stakes are extra stakes that lie beside the main stakes to make the basket stronger.

☐ Cut one bye-stake for each stake, 41cm (16″) long of No.8 (3mm) cane. Make a point at one end of each and insert them into the waling, one on the right of each stake. They must lie in the same channel as the main stake. Use the bodkin to help form a passage for them to slip into (fig.10).

Randing is a weave for economy and speed. It is very easy and only one weaver is used at a time.

☐ Put a weaver of No.5 (2.5mm) cane into any space and weave to the right, in front of one pair and behind one pair. Continue all the way round. There is no step-up in randing (fig.11).

Shaping. You must concentrate on the shaping. Every time a weaver goes round the front of a stake, hold that stake with the thumb and forefinger of the left hand. As you want the sides of the basket to go up straight you must hold the stake upright.

To join in a new weaver leave the old one at the back of a stake and place the new one against the same stake at the back (fig.12a).

Leave the ends until the siding is

finished and then trim off with a slanting cut so that they won't catch on anything in the basket (fig.12b).

☐ Rand for 9cm (3½″) keeping the sides quite straight.

☐ Wale for 3 rounds with No.5 (2.5 mm) cane and step-up as before.

Preparing for the handles. At this point start making room for the handles to fit into later.

☐ Cut 4 pieces of the handle cane about 23cm (9″) long, for liners, and slype one end.

Slyping is a special way to cut cane to a point. It is done by making cuts on 2 consecutive quarters of the cane (fig.13).

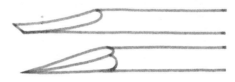

13. *A slype is made with two cuts.*

Slypes can be any length but start these 5cm (2″) from the end.

Insert 4 'handle liners' into the siding of the basket, beside 4 stakes and where you want your handle to be. Allow 8 stakes between the 2 liners on each side. Continue to weave round stake and liner together to form holes for the real handle.

☐ Rand for 2.5cm (1″) with sea-grass. You could substitute flat cane, raffia or No.5 (2.5mm) cane.

☐ Wale for 3 rounds with No.5 (2.5mm) cane.

☐ Rand for 2.5cm (1″) with sea-grass.

☐ Wale for 3 rounds with No.5 (2.5mm) cane.

Trac border. The sides of this basket are finished with a trac border.

☐ Re-soak the stakes if necessary and start with any stake and refer to it as the 1st and the next one to the right as 2nd, and so on.

☐ Bend the first stake and bye-stake together, 4cm (1½″) up from the waling, with quite a sharp bend. Pass this pair behind the 2nd pair, in front of the 3rd, behind the 4th, in front of the 5th and tuck them to the inside of the basket behind the 6th pair (fig.14).

☐ Now bend the 2nd pair down, making sure that the elbow of the bend is exactly the same height as the first bend. Repeat the weaving as for the previous pair and tuck them in behind the 7th pair.

☐ Repeat with each pair in turn and finish in exactly the same way, although you will weave the last few in front and behind stakes that have already been turned down. Be sure to keep them all in the correct order and don't let any cross over any others. Go in front of and behind the handle liners, together with the adjacent stake, and keep the pattern correct.

☐ Trim all ends of the weavers and the stakes with a diagonal cut so that they do not stick out. The border stake ends must lie against a stake or they will slip through to the front.

☐ Cut 2 pieces of prepared handle cane each 65cm (26″) long and slype all the ends. Bend into U-shapes. Remove the handle liners and keep them as they can be used again. Insert the handles well down into the spaces so the weaving grips them tightly. The handles should be about 13cm (5″) high.

☐ Insert a length of prepared wrapping cane, wrong side uppermost, into the siding, just under the border and to the immediate right of one of the handles. It should protrude 15cm (6″) to the inside (fig.15).

☐ Bring this short, protruding end up and over the top of the border, then down and across in front of the handle and the border. Re-insert it into the siding again just under the border, but this time to the left of the handle. Bring this same end up to lie behind the handle where it will be bound later.

☐ Cut a piece of enamelled cane (or wrapping cane), 41cm (16″) long, and insert it into the siding so that it lies against the outer curve of the handle, right side out. Use a peg to keep it in place temporarily (fig.16).

☐ Take the long end of the wrapping cane up and across the handle and the border so that a cross is formed in front of the border. Wrap this long end round the handle 4 times, binding in both the short end and the enamelled cane.

Continue to wrap the handle tightly but pass it over and under the enamelled cane to form a pattern (fig.17). This is not only decorative but helps to keep the wrapping tight. This handle was wrapped under twice and over twice but you can make any pattern you like.

☐ Continue wrapping handle, keeping the enamelled cane at the top and finish as you began with 4 plain wraps and a cross in front of the border to match the other end. Weave the end in and out of the waling to secure it.

☐ If you need to join in a new piece of cane lay the new cane, wrong side out, underneath the handle, when there is still enough of the old wrapping left to do another 5cm (2″). Continue to wrap with the old cane, binding the new cane in, until there is only 4cm (1½″) left of the old piece. Turn the new piece so that the right side is on the outside and commence wrapping with it. At the same time lay the old piece on the underside of the handle and bind it in with the wrapping.

☐ The handles need to be secured with a peg so that they will not slip out

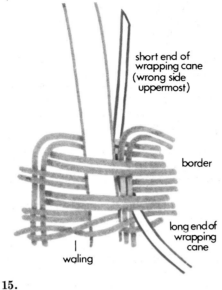

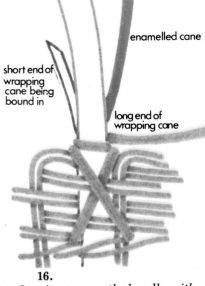

15.

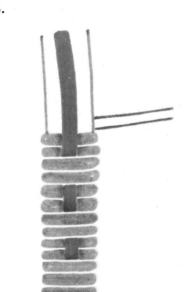

17.

15. *Starting to wrap the handle, with the wrapping cane in position.*
16. *Wrapping the handle.*
17. *Side view of handle wrapping showing the weaving over and under the enamelled cane.*

from the basket. While the handle cane is still wet, pierce it with a bodkin between the first and second rounds of the top waling.

☐ To make the peg point a short piece of No.10 (3.35mm) cane, or a wedge of the handle cane, and insert it into the hole made by the bodkin. It must come right through to the inside. You may have to tap it in with a hammer.

Cut this peg off, on the inside and the outside of the basket, level with the waling. This forms a peg which prevents the handles from slipping out.

Repeat on the other 3 places where the handles enter the sides.

☐ Finish the basket by shaping the handles. Make them curve towards each other by tying them together at the top while they are still wet. At the same time keep the sides of the basket apart by placing a book or a block of wood inside at border level. Leave it in position until the handles are dry.

Table mats and cheese platter

The inside or centre of a table mat is the beginning of most baskets, regardless of size or shape. To become familiar with the making of the centre—ie a woven base – and the technique of pairing, make these attractive mats in various sizes.

To make the table mats

Cane place mats look handsome on any table—they're good insulators and they thrive on being scrubbed clean with water—not soap. And you'll be thrilled at the cost.

To make 6 mats of 19cm ($7\frac{1}{2}''$) diameter or 4 mats of 24cm ($9\frac{1}{2}''$) or 10 mats of 12.5cm (5") diameter:

You will need:
170gm (6oz) No.5 (2.5mm) cane.
113gm (4oz) No.3 (2mm) cane.
283gm (10oz) No.8 (3mm) cane.

Tools
Side-cutters—you can use garden secateurs instead.
A bodkin—you can use a medium size knitting needle instead.

To make 19cm ($7\frac{1}{2}''$) mat

☐ Cut 8 pieces of No.8 (3mm) cane 17cm ($6\frac{1}{2}''$) long. These are for the base sticks which form the spokes of the mat. Point 4 of them at one end, and make a split of about 2.5cm (1") in the centre of the other 4. Use the bodkin to form the split. Thread all 4 of the pointed sticks into the split sticks so that they form a cross (fig.1).

☐ Bend a length of prepared (ie soaked in hot water for about 20 minutes) No.3 (2mm) cane roughly in the middle. Make this bend quite sharp. If the cane will not bend without cracking, twist it with the thumbs and forefingers of both hands held closely together. Twist each hand in opposite directions until the fibres of the cane give way. Loop this bend around one 'arm' of the cross and bring both ends to the front (fig.2).

These 2 ends of cane form 2 weavers and will now be referred to as the left-hand weaver and the right-hand weaver.

Pairing. Take the left-hand weaver in front of the same arm, over the top of the other weaver, round the back of the next arm and then to the front again as shown in fig.3.

☐ Repeat with the other end: across in front of one arm, over the other weaver and round the back of the next arm (fig.3).

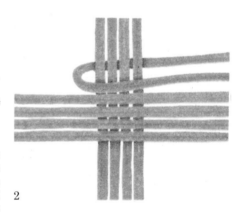
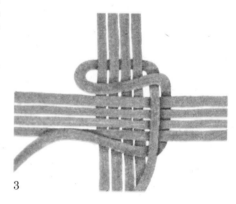

1

2

3

This is called pairing and is nearly always used for round and oval bases. Basically it's 'in front of one and behind one' and you should turn the work around with each stroke.

☐ Continue in this way until you have gone right round twice.

☐ On the 3rd round the arms must be opened into pairs. Instead of going right round the back of each arm, on the second part of the stroke bring the weaver to the front in between the middle two, making 2 pairs (fig.4).

1. The base of the mat is formed by a cross made of two sets of four sticks.
2. First steps in pairing.
3. Pairing continued.

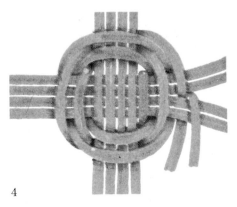

4

Repeat all the way round so that you have 8 pairs evenly spaced (fig.5).

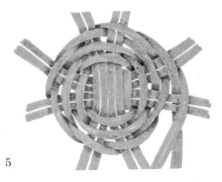

5

□ Weave in the same way for another 2 rounds, making 5 rounds in all, then open all the sticks on the next round so that they are all single (fig.6).

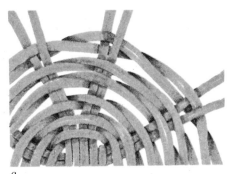

6

7

Joining. If you need to join in a new piece of cane, wait until the old one is on the outside. Pull it back with your left thumb and slip the new cane into the work so that it lies between this end and the work. The old end will protrude to the front and the new one to the back (fig.7).

□ Continue to pair until the work has a diameter of 9cm (3½"). Secure the pairing by threading the weavers under one cane of the previous round.

□ Join in 3 weavers of No.3 (2mm) cane. This can be done in two ways: a) they can be laid in 3 consecutive spaces or b) they can be inserted into the weaving down by the side of 3 consecutive sticks and then bent down to the front (fig.8).

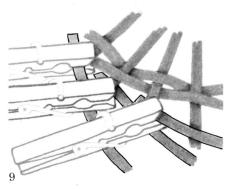

8

If you use method a) clip the ends down with a clothes peg until you have woven over them (fig.9).

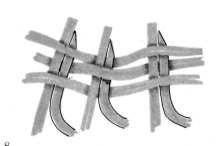

9

□ Put on 3 rounds of waling with these 3 weavers. Step up after each round and finish off ends.

□ Pair for 4 rounds.

□ Wale for another 2 rounds.

□ Trim all the ends of the weavers close to the work and cut off any surplus stick ends protruding beyond the weaving.

To make a trac border. Cut 32 border stakes of No.5 (2.5mm) cane 31cm (12") long. Soak them in hot water for 10 minutes. Point one end of each stake.

□ Insert one stake into the weaving on both sides of every stick. Insert the pointed ends and push them right down as far as they will go. Use the bodkin to form a channel for the stakes to slip into.

□ Put on a trac border. Bend each pair of border stakes in turn down to the right about 2.5cm (1") beyond the waling. Pass them behind the next pair, in front of the next, then behind and in front again. Tuck them into the back

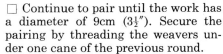

4. *On the third round, the cross is opened to form the spokes.*
5. *The cross opened to form eight pairs.*
6. *The pairs opened to single spokes.*
7. *Joining a new piece of cane.*
8. *Inserting cane for waling.*
9. *Using clothes pegs to hold cane.*

Opposite: this simple woven base is the starting stage for most baskets, and makes an elegant cheese platter. Designed by Barbara Maynard.

of the work in the next space. Repeat all the way round. The last few pairs will weave in and out of stakes that are already bent down.

☐ Trim the ends of the stakes with a diagonal cut so that the ends lie snugly and safely against a stake. Do not cut them too short or the ends will slip through to the front; if they are too long they will catch on to things and make the mat unstable.

To make 24cm (9½″) mat

You will need the same materials as before. The same quantity of cane will make 4 mats of this size.

The instructions are similar to the previous ones but the measurements and numbers differ slightly.

☐ Cut 10 pieces of No.8 (3mm) cane 20cm (8″) long.

☐ Split 5 of these in the centre with the bodkin and point the other 5 at one end. Thread the pointed pieces through the split to form a cross.

☐ Using prepared No.3 (2mm) cane, pair for 2 rounds.

☐ On the third round open the arms in 2 pairs with an odd one in the middle. Each arm will now be split into 2,1,2, (fig.10).

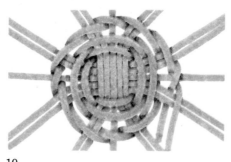

10

10. *Opening the cross to form spokes.*

☐ Pair for 3 rounds and then open the sticks into singles.

☐ Continue pairing until the work measures 11cm (4½″) in diameter.

☐ Put on 2 rounds of waling, 5 rounds of pairing and then a further 2 rounds of waling.

☐ Trim the ends of the weavers and cut off any surplus sticks protruding beyond the waling.

☐ Cut 40 pieces of prepared No.5 (2.5mm) cane 31cm (12″) long.

☐ Point one end of each piece and insert this end into the weaving of the base, one each side of each stick. .

☐ Put on a trac border and trim all the surplus ends.

To make 12.5cm (5″) mat

The same quantity of materials as before will make 10 small mats.

☐ Cut 6 base sticks of No.8 (3mm) cane 15cm (6″) long and thread 3 pointed ones into 3 split ones to make a cross (see fig.1).

☐ Pair for 2 rounds with No.3 (2mm) cane.

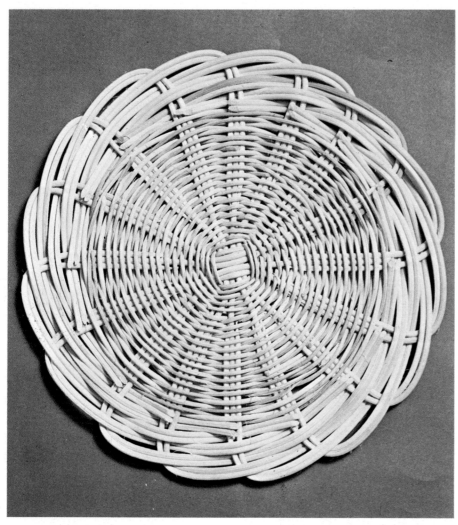

The wrong side of the mat shows the ends of the cane lying against the spokes. The cane must not be cut too short or the ends will slip to the front.

General hints

To help you to make a neat, closely woven base follow these hints:

Make quite sure that the left weaver passes over the top of the other one on its way to the back. Never leave one of the weavers at the back of the work—it must return to the front before you use the next one.

If you hold the base too tightly in your left hand it will curl up towards you. Try to hold it loosely and, in this case, flat.

If you find that the rounds of weaving have a gap between them, try pulling each weaver down hard when it is at the back of the work and then merely slip it to the front. Don't pull down when the weaver is to the front as this will distort the sticks and make the mat bend upwards. When you are ready to divide the sticks out, pull them apart with both hands and slip the weaver in between. Don't make the mistake of trying to make the weaver divide them.

☐ Open all the sticks to singles on the 3rd round and continue to pair until the work measures 6cm (2½″).

☐ Wale for 2 rounds. Trim weavers and sticks.

☐ Cut 24 border stakes of No.5 (2.5 mm) cane and put on a trac border, finishing as before.

The cheese platter

For a cheese platter 38cm (15″) in diameter thicker cane is used, as the larger a piece of work is, the thicker and stronger the cane must be. The techniques are similar to those used for making the smaller mats.

You will need:

57gm (2oz) No.10 (3.35mm) cane.

57gm (2oz) No.5 (2.5mm) cane.

57gm (2oz) No.8 (3mm) cane.

☐ Start with 12 base sticks of No.10 cane 34cm (12½″) long. Soak them for about 20 minutes. Pierce 6 in the centre and point one end of the other 6.

☐ Thread the pointed ones through splits to form a flat cross. If the sticks bunch together make the splits larger so that they remain flat.

☐ Bend a length of prepared No.5 (2.5mm) cane in the centre and loop it around one arm of the cross.

☐ Pair for 2 rounds, keeping the sticks of each arm together.

☐ On the 3rd round open the sticks into 12 groups of pairs, evenly all round the base.

☐ Put on 4 more rounds of pairing then open the sticks into singles.

☐ Continue pairing until the work measures 14cm (5½″) in diameter. Join in new lengths of prepared cane as needed.

☐ Wale for 2 rounds, pair for 4 rounds, wale for 2 rounds, pair for 4 rounds, wale for 2 rounds.

☐ Trim all the surplus ends of the weavers and sticks.

☐ Cut 48 pieces of No.8 (3mm) cane 51cm (20″) long. Point one end of each piece.

☐ Insert them into the weaving of the base, one on each side of each base stick. Insert them as far as the waling nearest to the centre to make a distinctive pattern.

☐ Put on a trac border. Bend a pair down to the right 4.5cm (1¾″) beyond the waling. Weave this pair behind and then in front of the next stakes 3 times, and then tuck it to the back in the next space.

☐ Repeat with each pair of stakes in turn. The last few will weave behind and in front of stakes that are already bent down. Make sure that each pair is bent down exactly the same distance from the weaving and that the work is even.

☐ Trim the ends of the stakes diagonally so that the ends lie snugly and safely against a stake.

Baskets and tiered platters

In basketry the designs are endless and once you have mastered the basic weaving techniques it is possible to make any number of articles without ever repeating the same design.

Basketry techniques can be used to make a variety of objects. The baskets illustrated here can be used in different ways and are easy to make. They make eye-catching party dishes for crisps, nuts and potato sticks or you can use them as platters to hold flat oven dishes.

If you are really ambitious you can join them together to make a tiered stand for a festive floral arrangement which is also sturdy enough to be heaped with fruit and nuts.

To make the baskets

Instructions are for three baskets with diameters of 18cm (7″), 25cm (10″) and 35.5cm (14″) which can be made into a stand.

You will need the tools and techniques which you have already used to make the first two projects.

Materials
57g (2oz) No.10 (3.35mm) cane.
113g (4oz) No.4 (2.25mm) cane.
170g (6oz) No.5 (2.5mm) cane.
113g (4oz) No.8 (3mm) cane.
57g (2oz) No.12 (3.75mm) cane.
113g (4oz) No.3 (2mm) cane.
113g (4oz) No.13 (4mm) cane (for tiered stand only).
Prepare, ie soak, the cane before starting the baskets.

The 25cm (10″) basket

Use No.10 (3.35mm), No.3 (2mm), No.4 (2.25mm) and No.5 (2.5mm) cane.

☐ Cut 8 base sticks of No.10 (3.35mm) cane 20cm (8″) long. Make a point at one end of four of the pieces. Using the bodkin split the other four in the centre and insert the pointed sticks into the split to form a cross. If the sticks bunch up then the splits are not long enough.

☐ Bend a length of prepared No.3 (2mm) cane—not quite centrally or the two ends will then be used up at the same time. To bend the cane break the fibres by twisting them with the fingers.

☐ Loop the cane where you have bent it over one 'arm' of the cross and bring both ends down to the front to form two weavers.

☐ Pair for 2 rounds keeping all the sticks of each arm together.

☐ On the third round open the arms of the cross into pairs. Don't expect the weaving to open the sticks. You have to pull the sticks apart with your fingers to get the correct shape.

☐ Continue to pair for 4 more rounds.

☐ Open the sticks so that they are all single like the spokes of a wheel.

☐ Continue pairing until the work has a diameter of 15cm (6″), joining in new weavers when necessary.

☐ Insert 3 lengths of No.4 (2.25mm) cane into any 3 consecutive spaces. Mark the stick immediately to the left of the left hand weaver.

☐ Wale for 3 rounds. Remember to do a step-up each time you reach the marked stick.

☐ Complete the 3 rounds of waling up to the marked stick. Then take the left hand weaver in front of 2 sticks and behind the marked stick and back to the front.

☐ Take the next weaver on the left in front of two sticks, behind one but thread it under the top weaver of the previous round on its way to the front.

☐ Repeat with the last weaver but thread it under the top weavers of the previous rounds on its way to front.

☐ Trim all surplus ends of sticks.

☐ Cut 64 stakes of No.5 (2.5mm) cane 30.5cm (12″) long and point one end of each stake.

☐ Insert the pointed ends of the stakes into the work. Insert two stakes on each side of each base stick.

☐ Insert two weavers of No.3 (2mm)

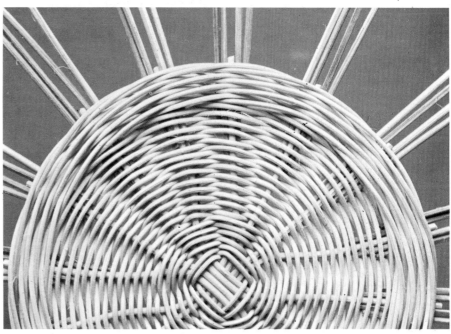

Additional stakes are added to the base for putting on the border

cane into the base weaving and pair for 4 rounds keeping the stakes in pairs. **To shape the bowl** wale for another 3 rounds but as you work gradually push the stakes up and away from you and weave in this position keeping the stakes in pairs. Remember to step-up on each round when waling. Finish as before.

The border. Starting with any pair of stakes bend them down to the right about 4cm (1½″) from the waling. Pass them behind the next two pairs, in front of the next two pairs, behind two pairs and back to the front which is the underside of the bowl (fig.1). While you are making the border try to bend the sides up and away from you to complete the bowl shape.

☐ Repeat with each pair of stakes in turn. The last few stakes will pass in front and behind stakes that are

Left: these versatile platters with sloping sides have intricate borders. Designed by Barbara Maynard.

already turned down. Keep the pattern correct and the stakes in their correct position. When you are finished you should not be able to see where you started and where you finished.

☐ Trim all surplus ends. Be careful not to cut border stake ends too short or they will slip through to the inside.

The 18cm (7") basket
Use No.8 (3mm), No.3 (2mm), No.5 (2.5mm) and No.4 (2.25mm) cane.

☐ Cut 6 base sticks of No.8 (3mm) cane 13cm (5") long.

☐ Pierce three in the centre and split them. Point one end of the other three and insert them into three split sticks to form a cross.

☐ Bend a length of prepared No.3 (2mm) cane and pair for 2 rounds before opening the sticks singly.

☐ Continue to pair until the work measures 9cm (3½") across.

☐ Wale for 2 rounds stepping up on the first round and finishing as before on the second round.

☐ Trim the surplus ends.

☐ Cut 48 stakes of No.5 (2.5mm) cane 25cm (10") long.

☐ Point one end of each stake and insert the pointed ends into the work—two on each side of each base stick.

☐ Insert two weavers of No.4 (2.25mm) cane and pair for 3 rounds keeping the pairs together.

☐ Insert three lengths of No.4 (2.25mm) cane and wale for 2 rounds shaping the bowl as before.

☐ Complete the bowl by putting on the same border as before and try to keep shaping the basket as you work.

The 35.5cm (14") basket
Use No.12 (3.75mm), No.4 (2.25mm), No.5 (2.5mm) and No.8 (3mm) cane.

☐ Cut ten sticks of No.12 (3.75mm) cane 23cm (9") long. Pierce five in the centre and point one end of the other five. Insert the pointed sticks into the split to form a cross.

☐ Pair for 2 rounds with No.4 (2.25mm) cane.

☐ Open the arms of the cross out to the pattern of 2-1-2 on each arm.

☐ Pair like this for 6 rounds and then open out into single sticks.

☐ Continue to pair until the work measures 20cm (8") across.

☐ Finish off the pairing and trim the ends of the weavers.

☐ Insert 3 lengths of No.5 (2.5mm) cane and wale for 3 rounds stepping up on the first 2 rounds and finishing as before on the third round.

☐ Cut 80 stakes of No.8 (3mm) cane 35.5cm (14") long and point one end of each. Insert the pointed end into the work—two on each side of each base stick—as before.

☐ Insert 2 lengths of No.4 (2.25mm) cane. Keep the stakes double and pair for 8 rounds bending the work up and away from you to shape the bowl.

☐ Insert 3 lengths of No.5 (2.5mm) cane and wale for 3 rounds stepping up on the first two rounds and finishing on the third round.

☐ Put on the same border as before but this time bend each pair of stakes down 4.5cm (1¾") from the waling. It is a bit more difficult to make this border as you are working with No.8 (3mm) cane. Soak the work well and keep shaping it as you work. Trim off the surplus ends.

The tiered stand
If you have made the three baskets and want to stack them don't be put off because it looks difficult. The stand is 38cm (15") high and made from No.13 (4mm) and No.5 (2.5mm) cane.

☐ Cut 10 stakes of No.13 (4mm) cane 51cm (20") long and point one end of each piece. Soak well—at least 30 minutes in hot water. These stakes will pass through the 3 baskets and the ends will be used to make a border underneath the large basket with a similar one on the top.

☐ Starting with the larger basket make 10 holes 5cm (2") from the centre. Use the bodkin to 'open' the work so that you do not damage the cane. Space the holes evenly to form a circle with a diameter of 10cm (4").

☐ Insert the stakes so that 7.5cm (3") protrudes from the wrong side of the basket.

☐ Wale for 2 rounds on the underside of the basket with No.5 (2.5mm) cane.
The footing. Using the short ends on the underside of the basket put on the foot border by bending each stake in

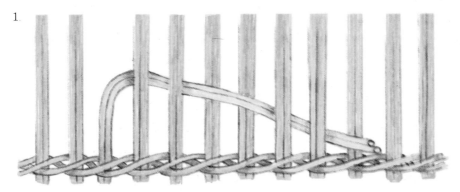

1. *Starting the border: bend the sides up and inwards to complete the shape.*

turn, down to the right, in front of one and then tuck it behind the next so that it is on the inside of the ring (fig.2). The last stake will have to be passed under a stake which has already been turned down.

☐ Turn the work the right way up and pull each stake in turn until the footing rests evenly on a flat surface.

☐ Wale with No.5 (2.5mm) cane on top side of basket for 4 rounds on the stakes stepping up on the first three rounds and finishing on the fourth.

Bye-stakes are inserted next to the stakes for additional strength.

☐ Cut 10 bye-stakes of No.13 (4mm) cane 19cm (7½″) long and point one end of each. Measure very accurately as they level the next basket.

☐ Insert the pointed ends of the bye-stakes into the waling, one to the right of each stake.

☐ 14cm (5½″) from the waling put on one round of fitching.

To fitch bend a piece of No.5 (2.5mm) cane roughly in the centre and loop it around a stake where the fitching is required. Let the two ends come to the front of the work to form two weavers.

☐ Grasp both weavers in the thumb and forefinger of the right hand and twist them towards you so that the right hand weaver comes over the top of the other.

☐ Slip the under one (or left one) round the back of the next stake and back to the front (fig.3). Repeat all the way round.

☐ Do not allow the circle of stakes to get wider while you are fitching. Keep the fitching level so that it is the same distance from the work all round.

☐ Insert another No.5 (2.5mm) cane and wale for 3 rounds stepping up on the first two rounds and finishing off on the third round.

☐ Make quite sure that all the bye-stakes are the same height. Trim them if necessary so that they are level with the waling. *Be careful not to cut any of the long stakes.*

☐ Use the bodkin and make 10 holes in centre basket to form a circle around the centre with a diameter of 7.5cm (3″).

☐ Thread the 10 stakes on the large basket through these holes and push the centre basket down on to the waling. Make sure that it is level.

2

2. Working the foot border.
3. Fitching: keep this level and same distance from work all round.
Ends protruding from bottom of large basket—first stage of tiered stand.

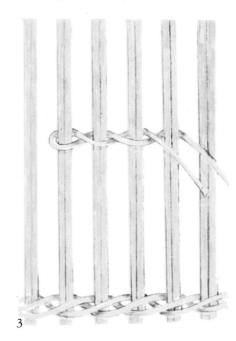

3

14

☐ Put 4 rounds of waling with No.5 (2.5mm) cane on to the stakes. Step-up on the first three rounds and finish on the fourth round.

☐ Cut 10 bye-stakes of No.13 (4mm) cane 16.5cm (6½″) long, point one end of each and insert the pointed end to the right of each stake and into the waling.

☐ Fitch as before 11.5cm (4½″) away from the waling and then insert another No.5 (2.5mm) cane and wale for 3 rounds. Trim the bye-stakes so that they are level and flush with the waling.

☐ Make 10 holes in the small basket to form a circle around the centre with a diameter of 5cm (2″).

☐ Thread the 10 stakes through these holes and push the basket down level on to the waling.

☐ Wale for three rounds with No.5 (2.5mm) cane on the top of the small basket.

☐ Use the stake ends to put on the same border as you did for the footing underneath the large basket. The tiered basket is complete when you have trimmed all the excess ends.

Mother and daughter shopping baskets

These lovely baskets are ideal for your next shopping expedition—one for you and one for your daughter. Beads can be added or if you prefer you can leave the baskets plain.

The instructions include many of the techniques that you have learned already as well as some new ones. Start with the smaller basket as it is easier to handle and to keep in shape.

When you have done this and are satisfied with the results you should feel confident enough to make the larger version. The larger basket will take longer. If the basket dries out and becomes difficult to handle you can always re-soak it.

The baskets
The smaller basket has a base diameter

Wooden beads are used to add colour to these shopping baskets for mother and daughter. Designer Barbara Maynard.

of 12.5cm (5"), height of sides, 11cm (4¼"). The larger basket has a base diameter of 20cm (8"), height of sides, 19cm (7½").

You will need:
For this project you will carry on with the same techniques and tools as the preceding chapters. You will also need a pair of round-nosed pliers.

Materials
The cane required for the baskets differs. As baskets get larger not only do they require more stakes but the cane must also be thicker to take the added weight.

The small basket
28g (1oz) No.3 (2mm) cane.
57g (2oz) No.5 (2.5mm) cane.
113g (4oz) No.8 (3mm) cane.

1m (39") No.10 (3.35mm) cane.
8mm (⅜") handle cane 61cm (24") long.
No.6 (2.6mm) chair seating cane, 5.5m (6yd) long.
61cm (24") enamelled wrapping cane—optional.
21 wooden beads with holes to fit No.8 (3mm) cane—optional.

□ Cut six base sticks of No.10 (3.35mm) cane, 13cm (5") long. Point one end of three pieces and split the other three. Make a cross.

□ Pair with No.3 (2mm) cane for two rounds and then open the four arms to single sticks.

□ Continue to pair until the work measures 11.5cm (4½") across. Instead of making the base quite flat try to curve it to form a slight dome. This gives great strength to the basket and will prevent the bottom from falling out.

□ Cut off any protruding base sticks and trim the surplus ends of the weavers.

□ Cut 23 stakes for the sides of No.8 (3mm) cane 40.5cm (16") long.

□ Slype (point) one end of each and insert a stake on each side of each base stick. Push the stakes into the weaving towards the centre. Note that there are 24 spaces and only 23 stakes are inserted. This is to get an odd number of stakes which makes randing easier. Leave the empty space where the base sticks are closest.

The upsett of a basket changes the direction at the base from going out to going up and it sets the shape for the rest of the basket whether it is straight up, flowing out, bowed or uneven. So, take great care with it. British baskets are nearly always upsett with waling.

□ Nip each stake close to the base with the round-nosed pliers(fig.1a)—make sure that the cane will bend easily and sharply without cracking. Nip the stakes in the correct direction to get them bending upwards.

□ Bend all the stakes up with the dome shape of the base up on the inside. Tie the stakes together at the top (fig.1b).

□ To continue with the small basket wale with 3 weavers (3 rod wale). Push three weavers of No.5 (2.5mm) cane into the pairing of the base alongside three consecutive stakes. The stakes are now used singly. Don't make the mistake of keeping them in pairs. Mark the stake immediately to the left of the first weaver so that you will know when to start the step-up on each round.

□ Wale for four rounds but on the first round try to make the waling as close to the pairing as possible otherwise there will be gaps in the basket. After the first round the waling will build up on top of the previous round.

1a. Nip cane with round-nosed pliers.

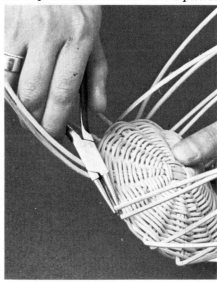

Don't forget the step-up on each round and finish off correctly.

☐ Untie the stakes and place a weight inside the basket to control the shaping more easily.

☐ Cut 23 bye-stakes of No.8 (3mm) cane 7.5cm (3″) long. Slype one end of each and insert one into the waling on the right side and in the same channel as each side stake.

☐ Rand with No.5 (2.5mm) cane for 5cm (2″) allowing the sides to lean out a little.

☐ Insert two 23cm (9″) handle liners, one on each side of the basket.

☐ Wale for two rounds with No.5 (2.5mm) cane and finish off if you are using beads. Cut off any surplus *bye-stakes* that protrude beyond the waling. If you are not using the beads wale for five rounds.

☐ Thread one bead on to each stake except the two where the handle liners are. Push them right down so that they are resting on the waling and are level all round.

☐ Wale on top of the beads for two rounds.

A rod border is a very neat and easily done border. It is sometimes called a commercial border because it is used more than any other by professional basket makers. Start with a three rod border—you can make thicker and bigger ones later.

☐ Re-soak the stakes and nip them with the round-nosed pliers 6mm (¼″) above the waling to make them bend down easily without cracking. Nip them so that they bend sideways to the right.

☐ Start the border anywhere you like. Bend a stake down to the right behind the next stake and back to the front. Repeat the same strokes with the next two stakes (fig.2).

☐ Go back to the first stake and pass it in front of the next upright stake and behind the next one and back to the front. Then bend the fourth stake down to the right to lie beside but behind the first stake (fig.3).

☐ Repeat these movements with the second and fifth stakes and the third and sixth stakes. You should now have three pairs of stakes at the front— one long and one short cane to each pair (fig.4).

☐ Counting the bent down ends find the fifth one from the right—it will be the right hand one of the last pair— and take it in front of the next upright and behind the next and back to the front (the same movement as before) and bend the next upright (the seventh) down to lie beside and behind it.

☐ Repeat all the way round the basket —fifth from the right in front of one and behind one, and the next upright down beside it until there is only one upright left (fig.5). Work round

the handle liners to make the border look as neat as possible.

☐ To finish the three rod border, again take the fifth from the right in front of one and under the elbow of the first cane and make the last upright bend down and under with it. You should still have three pairs to the front.

☐ The right hand stake of each of these pairs must be woven into the border in turn so that the border is complete and continuous. One stake comes to the front at each position all the way round. If you look at the top of the border where you began you will find that there are three single canes whereas all the rest of the rod border has two canes. Each of these single stakes has to have another cane lying with it and in front of it in order to complete the border.

☐ Take the fifth from the right and thread it under the elbow of the second stake that you bent down. Keep it in front of the first stake (fig.6).

☐ Now take the third from the right and thread it alongside (in front) of the next single cane and under the elbow of the third stake that you bent down.

☐ Lastly take the right hand one of the last pair and thread it alongside the last single cane and under the elbow of the fourth stake that you bent down.

There should now be one stake to the front evenly all the way round and these stakes should all be to the front at the bottom of the border. Make sure that the last three do not finish at the top of the border.

You may finish your border here if you wish. Clip off all the surplus cane very close to the border. But if you want your basket to look very neat add a second simple border. This is called a follow-on trac border.

A follow-on trac border is made by threading each border stake in turn into the inside of the basket one or two spaces to the right and just above the waling under the other protruding stakes (fig.7).

This forms a herring-bone pattern with the rod border and is very attractive. It has the added advantage that all the ends are inside the basket and won't catch on clothing, or scratch unprotected bare legs.

Trim the ends of these stakes on the inside but be careful that the ends lie against a stake. If you cut them too short they will slip through back to the front.

The handle

☐ Cut the handle cane to 53cm (21″) and soak it in hot water for 20 minutes.

☐ Slype both ends and shape the handle cane into a curve.

☐ Remove the handle liners and insert

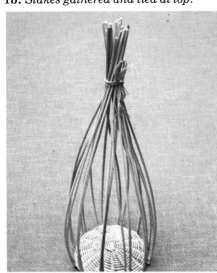

1b. *Stakes gathered and tied at top.*

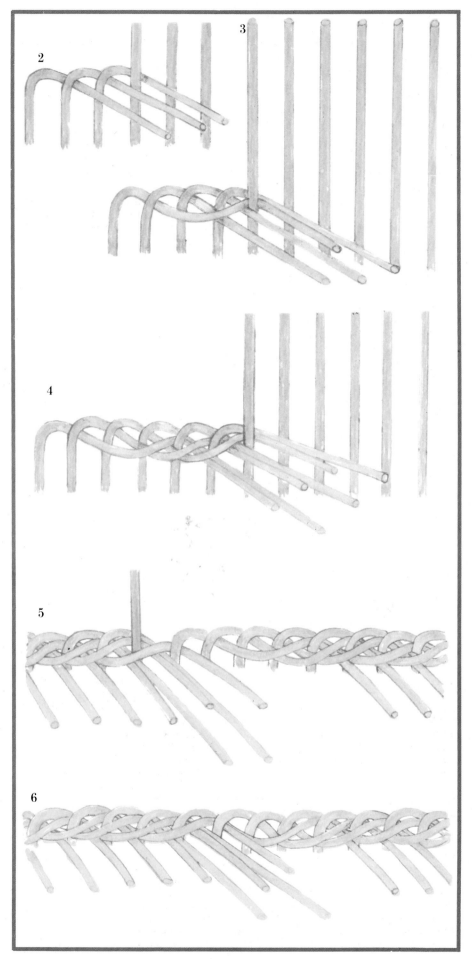

2. *First stage of 3-rod border.*
3. *The first rod passes behind the fifth to form a pair with the fourth.*
4. *Three pairs of stakes are formed to the front of the work.*
5. *The border is nearly complete and only one upright cane is left.*
6. *Remaining canes are passed under canes which are already bent down.*

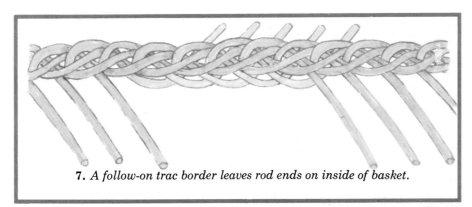

7. A follow-on trac border leaves rod ends on inside of basket.

The rod border as seen from above. The pattern is continued all the way round.

the bow into the holes made by the liners.

☐ Wrap the handle with No.6 (2.6mm) chair seating cane using either the enamelled wrapping cane or a piece of chair seating cane to form a pattern across the handle.

☐ Finish the basket by pegging the handle.

The large basket
You will need:
57g (2oz) No.5 (2.5mm) cane.
113g (4oz) No.6 (2.6mm) cane.

113g (4oz) No.10 (3.35mm) cane.
No.12 (3.75mm) cane, 1.85m (2yd) long.
No.10 (3.35mm) handle cane, 1m (39″) long.
5.5m (6yd) glossy wrapping cane or 8.3m (9yd) No.6 (2.6mm) chair seating cane.
1m (39″) enamelled cane—optional.
29 wooden beads to thread on to No.10 (3.35mm) cane—optional.

☐ Proceed as for the smaller basket starting with eight base sticks No.12 (3.75mm) cane, 23cm (9″) long.

☐ Pair for two rounds with No.5 (2.5mm) cane and open the sticks into twos.

☐ Pair for another three rounds and open the sticks into singles.

☐ Continue pairing until the work measures 19cm (7½″) across.

☐ Cut 31 stakes of No.10 (3.35mm) cane, 53.5cm (21″) long.

☐ Stake up and nip the stakes then wale for five rounds with No.6 (2.6mm) cane stepping up after each round.

☐ Cut 31 bye-stakes of No.10 (3.35mm) cane, 15cm (6″) long and insert into the work as before.

☐ Rand for 10cm (4″) and insert handle liners.

☐ If you are not using the beads put on eight rounds of waling before making the border.

☐ Put on four rounds of waling with No.6 (2.6mm) cane if you are using the beads. Then thread on the beads after trimming the protruding bye-stake ends. Add four more rounds of waling.

☐ Make the trac border as before.

☐ Cut the handle cane 86.5cm (34″) long, soak and shape, slype both ends and insert into work.

☐ Wrap and peg as before to complete the basket.

A close-up detail showing the handle wrapping and the peg which secures it.

Oval flower basket and tray

Baskets can be made round, oval and square and the designs are infinitely variable.

Oval baskets are particularly versatile. A low oval basket, for example, is ideal for flowers or, instead of sloping sides, you can put a trac border on to the same base to make a table mat; then if made with higher sides it becomes a shopping basket.

But beware! Oval basketry is not easy, so practise with plenty of round baskets before you embark on this shape. Oval bases tend to twist, and reverse pairing has to be used as well as pairing to counteract the twist.

For oval work some of the base sticks are longer than others and the longer ones are always threaded through the shorter ones. Although the longer sticks are often wrapped before the weaving is started, this is not essential. So, if you find wrapping complicated leave it out for the time being.

This chapter introduces reverse pairing, 4-rod waling and a rope handle.

To make an oval base

The base measures 19cm x 30.5cm (7½"x12") and can be used for the tray, the flower basket and the shopping basket.

You will need:

You will be using the same tools and techniques as for previous projects.
No.13 (4mm) cane, 3m (10') long.
No.6 (2.6mm) chair seating cane, 1.25m (48") long.
No.5 (2.5mm) cane, 57gm (2oz).

☐ Cut 3 sticks 33cm (13") long and 8 sticks 23cm (9") long, all from No.13 (4mm) cane.

☐ Pierce the short sticks in the centre and thread the 3 longer ones through. Arrange the sticks as shown (fig.1).

Wrapping—this is optional and need not be done for your first few baskets.

☐ Wrap the long sticks with No.6 (2.6mm) chair seating cane. Thread a piece of chair seating cane, wrong side uppermost, into the splits of the short ends. This will become the underside of the basket (fig.2).

☐ Wrap the cane round the double outer sticks so that it forms a cross on the upper side of the base.

☐ Wrap the long sticks between the short sticks. See that there are the same number of wraps between each of the short sticks (fig.3).

☐ Finish with a matching cross at the other end and thread the end of the chair seating cane under the wrapping for a few centimetres (inches).

☐ Pair with No.5 (2.5mm) cane. Loop the cane round the long sticks at one end of the base (as for a round base). Pair round the base for 2 rounds and try to keep the work straight and not sloping to one side. Weave close to the base sticks all round.

☐ Open all the sticks to form single spokes and then continue to pair for a further 4.5cm (1¾").

Make the right side of the base concave and try not to let the work twist. Keep all the short sticks, except the 2 outer ones, straight.

Reverse pairing

☐ Insert 2 pieces of No.5 (2.5mm) cane into base to right of 2 consecutive base sticks where the pairing ended. Hold

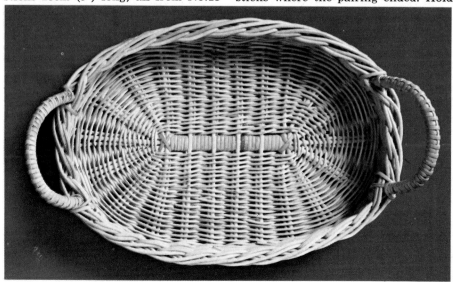

the 2 canes to back of work.

☐ Take the left hand weaver behind one stick and in front of the next—over the top of the other weaver—then to the back again. In other words, it is exactly the opposite of pairing. Each stroke must finish with both canes at the back (fig.4).

Join in a new cane in the same way as for pairing but push the new cane into position from the back so that the new end is at the front and the old one at the back (fig.5).

☐ Reverse pair for 4.5cm (1¾"). *The amount of reverse pairing must always equal the amount of pairing so that the twist is completely counteracted. The base should now measure 19cm x 30.5cm (7½"x12").*

☐ Trim all the ends of the weavers close to the work and also trim the protruding ends of the sticks.

This completes the base and you can add a trac border to make a table mat or continue and make a tray, flower basket or shopping basket. If you are inexperienced try the tray first.

To make the tray

The tray is the same size as the base, 19cm x 30.5cm (7½"x12") with sides 6cm (2¼") high plus the two handles (see previous page).

You will need:
(The materials include the cane needed for the base.)
No.13 (4mm) cane, 3m (10') long.
No.10 (3.35mm) cane, 85gm (3oz).
No.6 (2.6mm chair seating cane, 28gm (1oz).
No.6 (2.6mm cane, 57gm (2oz).
No.5 (2.5mm) cane, 57gm (2oz).
8mm (5⁄16") handle cane, 61cm (24") long.
Handle liners.

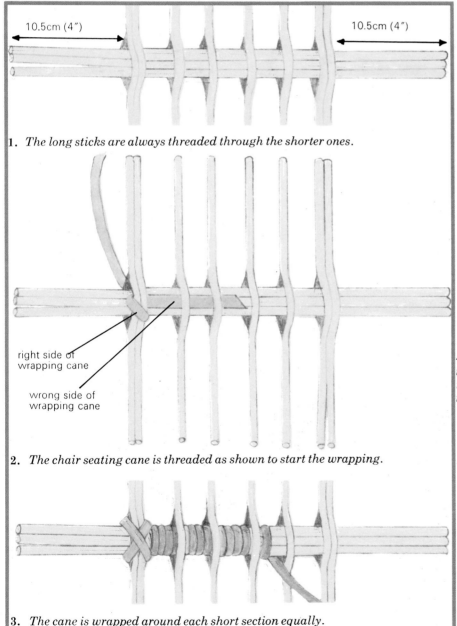

10.5cm (4")   10.5cm (4")

1. *The long sticks are always threaded through the shorter ones.*

right side of wrapping cane

wrong side of wrapping cane

2. *The chair seating cane is threaded as shown to start the wrapping.*

3. *The cane is wrapped around each short section equally.*

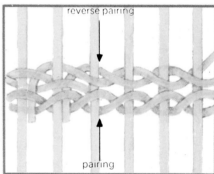

reverse pairing

pairing

4. *Reverse pairing is used to counteract the twist which occurs when pairing is used for oval work. The top row shows the cane inserted into the pairing.*

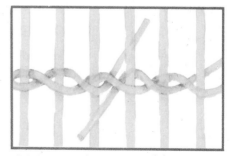

5. *Joining cane in reverse pairing.*

Left: these baskets are made with an oval base. The bases for both baskets are identical but the sides are different. Designer Barbara Maynard.

*Top: the canes are inserted next to
the handle cane to start the rope effect.*

*Right: once the handle is covered, each
cane is used separately and threaded
around the handle to create the herring-
bone pattern to finish the basket.*
*Above: detail of the rope handle showing
the inside view and the herring-bone
pattern on the outside.*

☐ Make the base as before.
☐ Cut 31 stakes of No.10 (3.35mm)
cane, 38cm (15″) long. Point one end of
each and insert them into the base in
the following order: one on each side
of each of the long sticks at both ends
and one on each side of each of the
outside short sticks at both ends, and
one beside each of the remaining short
sticks.

You will find that you are one stake
short. As for the round bases, one
stick is missing where the sticks are
closest, to give you an odd number.
☐ Nip the stakes close to the base and
bend them up with the dome shape of
the base uppermost.
☐ Tie the stakes together to keep them
in order while you upsett.
☐ Use 4 weavers of No.6 (2.6mm) cane
for this upsett as it needs to be sturdier
than for round baskets. Insert the
weavers into the base weaving beside
4 consecutive stakes, along one side of
the base.

4-rod wale by taking the left hand
weaver in front of 3 stakes and behind
one stake and back to the front. Use
each left hand weaver in turn. Try to
part the stakes at each end so that they
are all evenly spaced and make the
weavers go under the basket, close to
the pairing, before going behind the
next stake.
☐ Mark the stake to the left of the very
first weaver as you did for a 3-rod wale.
Wale all the way round until a weaver
passes round the marked stake.
☐ Cut this weaver off leaving about

15cm (6″) so that it can be woven to the
inside of the basket later.
☐ Step-up with remaining 3 weavers.
☐ Continue with a 3-rod wale—in
front of 2 and behind one—until the
sides measure 5cm (2″).
☐ Now thread the 4th weaver that you
cut off at the end of the first round,
into the inside of the basket. It will fill
a small gap.
☐ Put a weight inside the basket to
steady it. You will find it easier to
manipulate and shape the work.
☐ Insert 2 handle liners at each end of
the tray with 9cm (3½″) between each
pair.

A 4-rod border is exactly the same as
a 3-rod border except that you bend
down four stakes to the right, each
behind the next stake and back to the
front again. As you weave you will
always have 4 pairs to the front instead of 3 (for a 3-rod border) and at
the end there will be 4 weavers to
weave into the beginning of the border
instead of 3. If you are very ambitious
and skilful you can try a 5-rod border—
bend down 5 to start, always have 5
pairs and weave 5 away at the end.
The greater the number of rods, the
thicker and sturdier the border becomes. Use No.10 (3.35mm) cane.
☐ Put on a follow-on trac border if you
wish as it does give a neat finish.
☐ Cut 2 pieces of handle cane 30.5cm
(12″) long, soak well and curve them into bow shapes.
☐ Slype both ends of the bow so that
the cuts come on the inside of the bow.

24

☐ Remove handle liners and insert the handle. Wrap the handle and peg it to finish. The method for doing this is shown on pages 4 and 5.

Flower basket

Using the same base as before, the sides of this basket are 10cm (4″) high plus the rope handle.

You will need:

(The materials include the cane needed for the base.)

No.13 (4mm) cane, 3m (10′) long.
No.10 (3.35mm) cane, 113gm (4oz).
No.6 (2.6mm) chair seating cane, 1.25m (48″) long.
No.6 (2.6mm) cane, 113gm (4oz).
No.5 (2.5mm) cane, 113gm (4oz).
8mm ($\frac{5}{16}$″) handle cane, 66cm (26″) long.
Handle liners.

☐ Make an oval base exactly as before.
☐ Cut 31 stakes 48.5cm (19″) long of No.10 (3.35mm) cane.

Although this basket is only 5cm (2″) higher than the tray, it flows out more which means that the border stakes will be wider apart and the border will therefore need more cane.

☐ Insert the stakes into the base as for the tray.
☐ Nip the stake ends and upsett with a 4-rod wale for one round and continue with a 3-rod wale for 4 more rounds.
☐ Cut 31 bye-stakes of No.10 (3.35mm) cane, 12.5cm (5″) long, point one end of each and insert them into the waling—one to the right of each stake.
☐ Using No.6 (2.6mm) cane, rand for 7.5cm (3″) trying to bend the ends of the basket well out but keeping the sides straight up. Don't forget that a stone or weight in your basket will help to keep it steady and make it easier to shape the work.
☐ Put in handle liners, one on each side of the basket.
☐ Wale for 4 rounds still shaping the ends outwards.
☐ Put on a 3, 4, or 5-rod border and a follow-on trac border if you like.
☐ Cut one piece of handle cane 66cm (26″) long, shape into a bow and slype each end. Remove the handle liners and insert the handle.

Rope handle

☐ Cut 10 pieces of No.5 (2.5mm) cane 96.5cm (38″) long, point one end of each and insert 5 beside the handle bow at each end. Insert them into the top of

the border and to the left of the bow at each end. Try to make them follow the bow round.
☐ Start at one side and take that set of handle weavers across in front of the bow—to the right—then wrap them round the bow 3 or 4 times, over to the other side. Leave the ends of these canes inside the basket.
☐ Repeat with the other set of weavers on the other side, taking these weavers into the spaces between the first set. Take care to keep them all in the correct order and do not let them twist at all.
☐ When both sets of weavers are in place there may be gaps or 'grins' in between the canes. If so cut 2 more weavers and insert one on each side—to the right of the original set—and follow the roping effect as before. Repeat with 2 more if necessary.

If the handle gets filled up in places but not in others, it means that the initial roping was not even. Start again and have another go.
☐ Push all the weaver ends through the waling, from the inside to the outside of the basket and to the right of the handle bow underneath the waling. Again be sure to keep these weavers in the correct order.

To make the herringbone finish, these weavers have to be taken up and around the back of the handle and back to the front again. Use one weaver at a time.
☐ Hold the basket with one side towards you so that the ends of the weavers will be protruding on the right of the handle bow.
☐ Take the first (or left hand) weaver, up and across the waling, over the border on the left of the handle, round the back of the handle and back down and across the waling. Push this weaver to the inside of the basket on the left of the handle, again underneath the waling. Use each weaver in turn.

Make sure that the crosses all come even, each one higher than the last and as close to the handle as possible.

Weaving away—when all the weavers are inside the basket weave them in and out of the waling to finish them off. This is called weaving away.
☐ Repeat the herringbone pattern on the other side and weave away.

Shopping basket

A shopping basket is made by a combination of the 2 previous baskets. Make the base exactly as before.

Cut stakes 46cm (18″) long.

Upsett, wale, bye-stake, rand and top-wale as for the flower basket, but keep the sides quite straight. Put one handle liner at each end. Put on the same border as before and add the rope handle from end to end.

Left: wrapping the handle. Canes are passed around the handle cane to the opposite side.

A doll's cradle

A very pleasant way of learning new basketry techniques is to make the doll's cradle illustrated. The base for the cradle can be made exactly like the oval base described on page 21, or if you wish you can alter it, and learn a new technique.

The new techniques in this chapter are chain pairing, plait borders and packing. The chain pairing on the base is not essential but it is attractive and not at all difficult. The plaited border looks difficult but follow the instructions carefully and you will get it right the first time. Packing means building up one side of a basket so that it is higher than the rest.

The cradle

The cradle is 30cm (11¾") high and 37cm (14½") long. The rockers are not essential so if you can't work with wood don't let it put you off making the cradle.

You will need:

Tools and techniques as for previous basketry chapters.
57gm (2oz) No.13 (4mm) cane.
170gm (6oz) No.10 (3.35mm) cane.
57gm (2oz) No.5 (2.5mm) cane.
170gm (6oz) No.6 (2.6mm) cane.
No.6 (2.6mm) chair seating cane 1.83m (2yd), long.

For the rockers:

2 pieces of softwood 50mm x 25mm (2"x 1"), 28cm (11") long—optional.
4 No.10 brass screws 25mm (1") long with washers or screw cups to attach rockers to basket.
Surform tool to shape rockers.
Saw and fine grade glasspaper.

☐ Cut 3 sticks 33cm (13") long and 8 sticks 23cm (9") long, all from No.13 (4mm) cane, to make the base.
☐ Pierce and thread the sticks and wrap with chair seating cane as we have described on page 21.

Chain pairing

To prevent oval work from twisting, an equal number of pairing and reverse pairing rounds are put on the base. If these techniques are used on alternate rows they form a chain pattern.

☐ Working from a long end pair with No.5 (2.5mm) cane for half a round only.
☐ Loop a second weaver round next stick beyond the pairing and reverse pair until you reach the pairing weavers.
☐ Drop the reverse pairing weavers and continue pairing with the pairing weavers until you reach the reverse pairing weavers again. Continue in this way, alternating the pairs of weavers, and never letting either pair overtake the other. Keep the reverse pairing weavers at the back of the work and the pairing weavers to the front.

☐ Open all the sticks to singles on the third round and make the base slightly concave.
☐ Continue chain pairing until the work measures 19cm x 30.5cm (7½"x 12").
☐ Trim surplus weavers and sticks.
☐ For the upsetting you will need 31 stakes of No.10 (3.35mm) cane. These will differ in length. Half the number, say 15, must be shorter and will go round the foot of the cradle—cut these 51cm (20") long. The longer ones, the remaining 16, go round the hood and must gradually increase in length. Cut 2 lengths of each starting at 53.5cm (21") and then in increments of 2.5cm (1"). The length of these stakes varies according to how high and how far over you want the hood to be.
☐ Point one end of each stake and insert the pointed ends into the base. Make sure that the slight dome on the base will be inside the basket. Be careful to keep the longer ones together at one end and in the correct order and position for the hood.
☐ Nip each stake close to the base pairing, so that they bend up easily without cracking.
☐ Tie the stakes together in two bunches—one bunch at the foot and the other at the head. This is to make the upsetting easier and to avoid distorting the base.
☐ Insert 4 weavers of No.6 (2.6mm) cane into the base and do a 4-rod wale for one round. Change to a 3-rod wale for 5 rounds remembering to step-up on each round.
☐ Cut 31 bye-stakes of No.10 (3.35mm) cane, half of them 13cm (5") long and half gradually increasing, as for the stakes, to a maximum of 28cm (11").
☐ Point one end of each and insert the pointed ends into the waling of the upsetting, one beside, and to the right, of each stake. Keep the longest bye-stake beside the longest stake etc, in order, all the way round.
☐ Rand with No.6 (2.6mm) cane for 5cm (2"). Allow the sides to flow out a little and the ends slightly more.
☐ Using No.6 (2.6mm) cane put on two rounds of 3-rod waling.

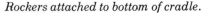

Rockers attached to bottom of cradle.

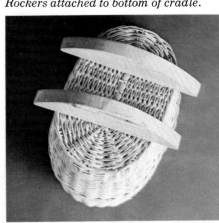

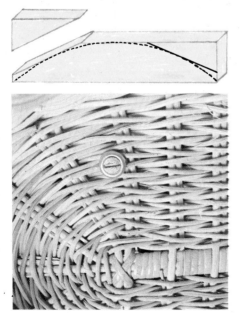

This cradle with its plait border involves new techniques and careful weaving. Designer Barbara Maynard.

1. To make the hood one side of the basket is packed. A weaver is taken round a decreasing number of stakes.

Above left: diagonal saw cuts remove waste. Corners are filed round.
Below left: detail of screws in position.

Packing—this is done to make the hood.

☐ Start randing with No.6 (2.6mm) cane, at the head of the cradle and weave to the right until you reach the middle of the side.

☐ Turn the weaver right round the next stake and weave back towards the head, all the way round, until you reach the middle of the other side.

☐ Turn the weaver right round the next stake so that it is facing the head

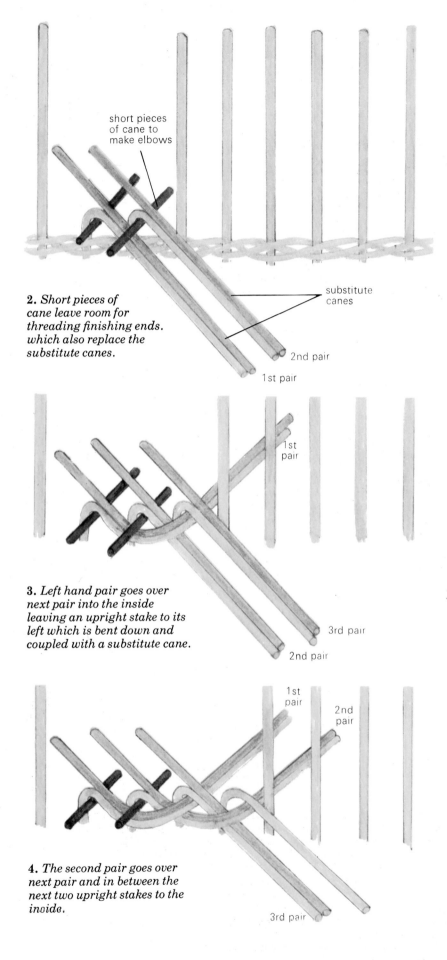

2. *Short pieces of cane leave room for threading finishing ends. which also replace the substitute canes.*

short pieces of cane to make elbows

substitute canes

2nd pair

1st pair

1st pair

3. *Left hand pair goes over next pair into the inside leaving an upright stake to its left which is bent down and coupled with a substitute cane.*

3rd pair

2nd pair

1st pair

2nd pair

4. *The second pair goes over next pair and in between the next two upright stakes to the inside.*

3rd pair

end again.

☐ Continue randing to the other side to one stake less than on the previous round.

☐ Turn the weaver round again and weave to the other side, again to one stake less than on previous round (fig. 1).

☐ Repeat this weaving backwards and forwards going round one stake less each time on both sides so that the head end grows higher. Push the stakes forwards as you weave to form the hood.

☐ Continue until you are turning the weaver round the two longest stakes. Leave the weaver on the inside of the work.

☐ Using No.6 (2.6mm) cane wale for two rounds all the way round the cradle and then repeat the packing procedure exactly as before. (For a bigger hood you can repeat the packing process a third time if you wish.)

☐ Finally put on two more rounds of waling using No.6 (2.6mm) cane.

☐ Trim any surplus *bye-stakes* and weavers—*not the stakes.*

You can now complete the cradle with a 3-rod border if you wish but a plait border is more decorative.

Plait border

Keep the work well soaked and if you make a mistake don't be discouraged, undo the work and try again, the result is well worth the effort.

☐ Using No.10 (3.35mm) cane cut 3 pieces 26cm (10″) long and 2 pieces 7.5cm (3″) long. The long canes are substitute stakes and will be replaced by the real ones at the end. The short canes are merely cushions so that the first canes are not bent down too low and will allow space to thread the last stakes under these 'elbows' at the end of the border.

☐ Nip all the stakes 6mm (¼″) above the waling so that they bend over easily to the right.

☐ Starting at the foot end (the easiest place) place one of the 7.5cm (3″) canes against a stake at right angles to the waling and bend the first stake down to the front over it. Place a 26cm (10″) substitute cane alongside the stake. Leave 5cm (2″) sticking into the inside.

☐ Repeat with the other 7.5cm (3″) cane against the next stake to the right and bend that stake down over it and place the second substitute cane behind it (fig.2).

☐ Take the first left hand pair over the second pair and in between the next two upright stakes, into the centre of the basket. Bend the third stake down to the front over this pair and place the third substitute cane beside and alongside this stake (fig.3).

☐ Take the second pair over the third pair and between the next two upright stakes into the centre. Bend the fourth stake down to the front (fig.4). Bring the left hand pair on the inside of the work back to the front to lie beside, but behind, the stake you have just bent down (fig.5).

☐ Repeat the last stroke with the third pair and once again the inside left hand pair is brought out to lie beside and behind the fifth stake (fig.6).

☐ From now on you will have 2 pairs on the inside. Always bring the left hand one out, after you have turned down the next stake. At the same time you will have 2 sets of 3 canes to the front. Counting these canes from the right, take the 5th and 6th cane each time, to the inside of the basket, in between the next two upright stakes, and over the top of the first 4 canes lying at the front.

Say to yourself, 'five and six go in, next stake down and left hand pair comes out'. If it goes wrong and you suddenly have a cane that is too short to complete its stroke, it is because you have twisted the canes round as you passed them in or out of the basket.

☐ Repeat all the way round making sure that you turn each stake down close to the waling. Don't leave gaps between the border and the waling. Continue until you have bent the last stake down and the left hand inside pair comes out.

To finish the border remove the first 7.5cm (3″) cane (if it has not already fallen out) and thread the fifth and sixth cane from the right under the elbow of the second stake (fig.7).

There are now 3 pairs on the inside— a long cane and a short cane to each pair. Each of the right hand canes (the long ones) is the real stake that is to replace each of the substitute ones. Keep them in the right order.

☐ Remove the left hand or first substitute cane bit by bit and weave the real cane into its place. Don't remove so much of the substitute cane at any one time that you lose the place where the real one goes (fig.8).

☐ Repeat this with the centre and remaining right hand canes.

☐ Now you have three odd canes on the inside of the basket. Thread each of these canes one 'plait' to the right and through the border to the front. The plaited border will now look continuous all the way round.

☐ Trim off the ends of the canes as close to the plait as possible.

To make the rockers saw the 2 pieces of wood with a diagonal cut at each end as shown in diagram on page 27.

☐ Round the corners off with a Surform.

☐ Smooth the curve with fine glasspaper.

☐ Decide on exactly the right position for the rockers and the screws to be attached to the cradle. For the screws

gouge holes 8.5cm (3⅜″) from each end of each rocker, on the upper flat surface, with a bodkin or a bradawl.

☐ Varnish the rockers.

☐ Push the screws through the screw cups or washers and then through the base weaving so that they match the holes in the rockers. Be careful not to split any of the base sticks or weavers with the screws.

☐ Tighten the screws to secure the rockers in position.

5. *The first pair goes over the second pair on its way to the front to lie next to the fourth stake.*

6. *The third pair goes to the inside and the second pair comes out over it to lie next to the fifth stake.*

7. *The short bits of cane are removed and now the real stakes must take the place of the substitute canes.*

the first
real stake
in position

8. *The first substitute cane is removed in stages and the longer stake of the pair is threaded into position.*

Wine cradles

The wine cradles illustrated are made with oval bases. The techniques involve packing one end to support the top of the bottle and a variation of it making a recess for the neck of the bottle. Two types of handles are made. The first type consists of two flexible curved handles and the other is a secure T-shaped handle. The completed cradles can be dyed or stained with wood stains if you wish.

You can design your own baskets. For example you can pack both ends of the oval base to make a fruit or flower basket. Make a cross handle and wrap it with chair seating cane or use cane for a rope effect.

Cradle with curved handles

The base of the cradle measures 17cm x 10.5cm ($6\frac{3}{4}''$x$4\frac{1}{4}''$) and after packing, it is 27cm ($10\frac{1}{2}''$) long.

You will need:

Tools and techniques as described in previous Basketry chapters.

28gm (1oz) No.3 (2mm) cane.

28gm (1oz) No.5 (2.5mm) cane.
57gm (2oz) No.6 (2.6mm) cane.
57gm (2oz) No.8 (3mm) cane.
No.10 (3.35mm) cane, 1.83m (2yd) long —for the base sticks.
8mm ($\frac{5}{16}''$) handle cane, 1m (1yd) long.
No.2 (1.85mm) chair seating cane, 1m (1yd) long—optional for wrapping the base sticks.
No.6 (2.6mm) chair seating cane, 5.5m (6yd) long—for handle wrapping.
Sticky tape.
All-purpose adhesive.

To make the base. Cut 6 sticks 11.5cm ($4\frac{1}{2}''$) long and 3 sticks 18cm (7") long, all from No.10 (3.35mm) cane.

☐ Pierce the short sticks in the centre and thread the long ones through to form an oval pattern with the short sticks grouped in the centre with a space of 1.6cm ($\frac{5}{8}''$) between each. Wrap the long sticks with No.2 (1.85mm)

chair seating cane – this is optional, but does give extra strength.

☐ Pair and reverse pair with No.3 (2mm) cane so that the base measures 15cm x 9.5cm (6"x3$\frac{3}{4}$"). Make the base slightly concave—the dome will form the inside of the basket.

Put on the pairing and the reverse pairing in any pattern, but use an equal number of rounds of each. Chain pair if you wish—it is very attractive

☐ Trim surplus base sticks once base weaving is completed.

Upsetting

☐ Cut 27 stakes of No.8 (3mm) cane, 16 of these must be 30.5cm (12"). Gradually increase the length of the remaining eleven to a maximum of 35.5cm (14"). This is for the forward end, or front, which juts out and is slightly higher than the rest of the basket.

☐ Point one end of each stake and insert them into the base so that the odd one out is a short stake at the back of the basket. The longer stakes are arranged round the front end with the longest stake in the centre.

☐ Nip the stakes close to the base weaving and bend them upwards. Tie them together at the top.

☐ Upsett with one round of 4-rod waling and continue with a 3-rod wale for 2 more rounds, all with No. 6 (2.6mm) cane. Step-up after each round.

☐ Cut 27 bye-stakes of No.5 (2.5mm) cane, 21 of these are 10cm (4") long and the remaining 6 are 30.5cm (12") long.

☐ Point one end of each and insert them into the upsetting, one on the right side of each stake. The longer bye-stakes must be arranged at the front with the longer stakes. These long bye-stakes will eventually become 'stakes' to help form the lip of the basket.

☐ Put on 10 rounds of randing with No.6 (2.6mm) cane. Keep the sides and the back going up vertically but ease the front stakes slightly forwards and outwards.

☐ Wale for 3 rounds with No.6 (2.6mm) cane still shaping the front of the basket.

☐ Put on 6 rounds of randing with No.5 (2.5mm) cane and keep shaping the front. Finer cane is used for this randing so that it is easier to shape the lip or front of the basket.

☐ On the next round of randing, divide the 6 long stakes and bye-stakes at the front, so that they become singles.

☐ Rand for 2 more rounds keeping the front stakes single and shaping the lip well to the front.

Packing

☐ Build up the lip by randing backwards and forwards with No.5 (2.5mm) cane. Start at the fifth stake from the

The blue wine cradle is dyed with wood stain. The cradle is made exactly like the one next to it but the handle is different. Designer Barbara Maynard.

Detail of packing to form lip.

centre of the back and weave towards the front, around the front to the fifth stake before the centre of the back. Bend the weaver right round this stake and weave back along the previous round but to one stake less than from where you started. Keep repeating this, randing backwards and forwards, one stake less each time on both sides, until you are only weaving round the last 2 stakes. Keep shaping the lip while doing this. Leave the end of the weaver on the inside of the basket.

☐ Wale all the way round with No.6 (2.6mm) cane for 2 rounds.

☐ Trim all the surplus ends of the *21 shorter bye-stakes*. Be careful not to cut off the 6 longer bye-stakes as they will be used for the border.

Border

☐ Re-soak the stakes if necessary and nip them 6mm ($\frac{1}{4}$″) above the waling. Put on a 4-rod border. Trim all the surplus stakes and weavers.

The handles

☐ Cut 2 pieces of 8mm ($\frac{5}{16}$″) handle cane 53.5cm (21″) long. Make a tongue at both ends of each by cutting away most of the thickness of the cane on one side (fig.1). Start the cuts 15cm (6″) in from the ends. Don't make the usual slanting cut but cut away quite

sharply and then straight down to form a tongue. Both cuts on each handle piece must face the same way.

☐ Soak the cane well and bend it to the shape you require. Push the two tongues into the basket from the outside and underneath the top waling. Position them as illustrated, near the fourth stake from the back and the front.

☐ Bend the tongues up and over the border to meet the main part of the handle (fig.2). Keep the 'eyelet' that is formed round by shaping it with your fingers or by bending it round the handle of a bodkin. Make sure both handles are the same length and height.

☐ Secure the tongues to the main part of the handles with sticky tape and leave the work to dry. Remove sticky tape and stick into position with all-purpose adhesive and secure again with sticky tape until dry.

☐ Wrap each handle with No.6 (2.6mm) chair seating cane. Bend this cane about 5cm (2″) from one end so that it forms an L-shape just above the eyelet, ie where the tongue joins the handle (fig.3).

☐ You are now ready to start wrapping with the long end. Put a piece of chair seating cane in the work to go over the

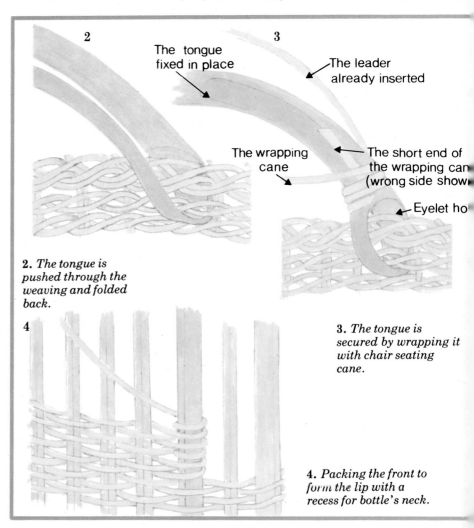

2. *The tongue is pushed through the weaving and folded back.*

3. *The tongue is secured by wrapping it with chair seating cane.*

4. *Packing the front to form the lip with a recess for bottle's neck.*

top of the handle and wrap it in with the short end around the handle. Continue wrapping, making any pattern you wish with the leader.

☐ Wrap across to the other side to the edge of the eyelet hole to finish with four plain rounds of wrapping.

☐ Finish by tucking the end back up inside the wrapping. This is done by loosening the wrapping and pulling the end through and then tightening the wrapping again. It can also be secured by pushing it through the join by the tongue and the handle and keeping it in position with all-purpose adhesive once the cane is dry.

☐ Repeat for the other handle.

Cradle with T-handle

The base for the cradle (shown here) is made exactly like the one for the previous cradle.

You will need:

28gm (1oz) No.3 (2mm) cane.
85gm (3oz) No.6 (2.6mm) cane.
57gm (2oz) No.8 (3mm) cane.
No.10 (3.35mm) cane, 1.83m (2yd) long —for the base sticks.
No.2 (1.85mm) chair seating cane, 1m (1yd) long—optional for wrapping the base sticks.
No.6 (2.6mm) chair seating cane, 5.5m (6yd) long—for handle wrapping.
8mm ($\frac{5}{16}$″) handle cane, 1.22m (48″) long.
Handle liners, 3.
All-purpose adhesive.
1 small panel pin or nail.

☐ Make the base as before.

☐ Upsett and continue as for the previous cradle until you have to cut the bye-stakes.

☐ Cut 27 bye-stakes of No.8 (3mm) cane—16 must be 10cm (4″) long and the remaining eleven must gradually increase to a maximum length of 18cm (7″). Point one end of each and insert them into the waling, one on the right side of each stake. Arrange them so that the longer ones áre at the front and in the correct order.

☐ Rand for 10 rounds with No.6 (2.6mm) cane.

☐ Insert the handle liners, one in the centre back and the other two—one on either side—at the sixth cane from the front. These 2 must be more than half-way towards the front to balance the basket when tipped to pour the wine.

☐ Cut 2 pieces of 8mm ($\frac{5}{16}$″) cane 15cm (6″) long. Point one end of each and soak them well.

☐ Insert these 2 sticks into the weaving at the front to form the edges of the

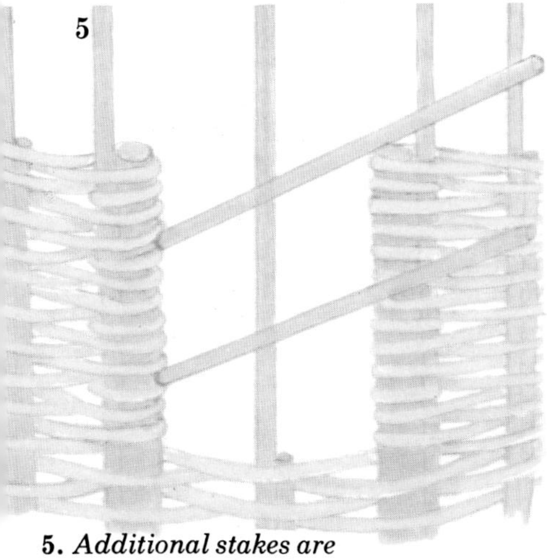

5. *Additional stakes are inserted for the border.*

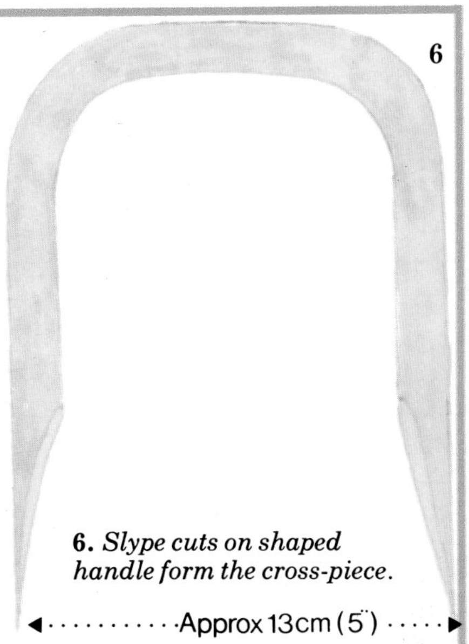

6. *Slype cuts on shaped handle form the cross-piece.*

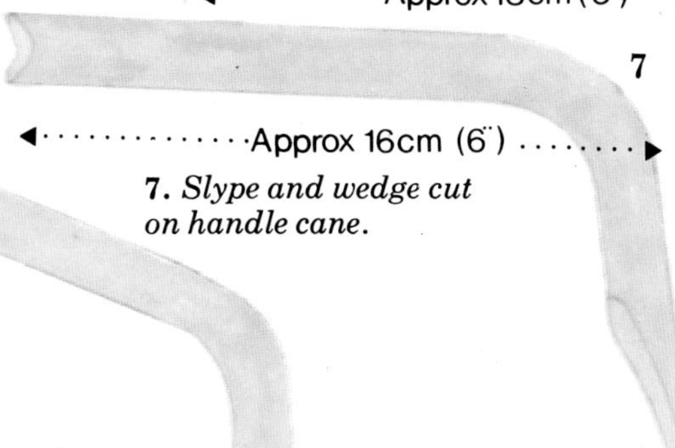

◄ · · · · · · · · · · · Approx 13cm (5″) · · · · · ►

1. *The handle cane is cut as shown to form a tongued shape.*

◄ · · · · · · · · · · · Approx 16cm (6″) · · · · · · · ►

7. *Slype and wedge cut on handle cane.*

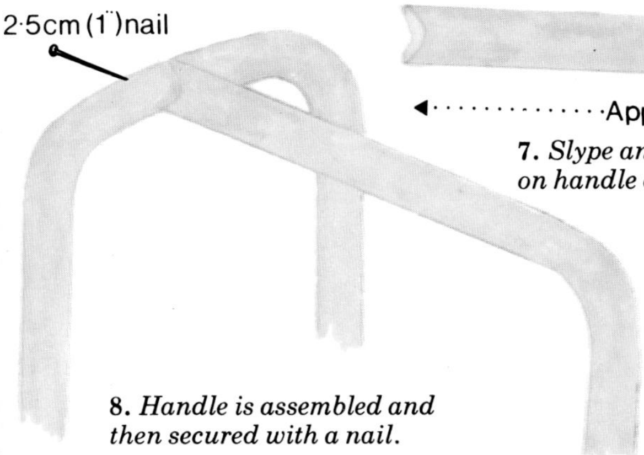

2·5cm (1″)nail

8. *Handle is assembled and then secured with a nail.*

Above: wine cradle with recess to hold the bottle's neck. The handle is similar to that of the blue cradle.

opening. Insert them next to the 2 stakes that are immediately to the left and right of the centre stake so that only one stake is left in the middle. Remove and discard the bye-stakes if necessary to insert the sticks more readily.

☐ Bend the sticks well forward into the shape that you intend for the opening.

☐ Rand with No.6 (2.6mm) cane all the way round for 9 rounds. Press the front stakes forwards.

Packing

☐ Build up the front as before, but this time leave a gap in the work. Start as before at the fifth stake from the back and rand as far as the thick stick at the front. Wind the cane round that stick and back along the same side to one stake less. Every other time you pass the thick stick pass the cane round it twice so that it builds up well and completely covers the stick (fig.4).

☐ Continue like this until you are weaving round the last two stakes. Leave the cane on the inside of the work.

☐ Repeat on the other side and make sure both sides are the same height.

☐ Put on 4 more rounds of randing on each side by working backwards and forwards. The gap at the front should now be about 4.5cm (1¾") deep.

☐ Insert 3 weavers of No.6 (2.6mm) cane next to the first three stakes next to the gap at the front. Wale right round to the other side, cut off the weavers and insert the ends into the

weaving.

☐ Cut off all the surplus bye-stakes including the one at the front in between the two thick sticks.

☐ Re-soak the two thick sticks if necessary and cut them off so that they are level with the weaving.

Plait border

☐ Cut 4 pieces of No.8 (3mm) cane, 20cm (8") long and point one end of each. These are border stakes for the gap. Insert 2 into each thick stick one 13mm (½") from the top and one 13mm (½") from the bottom of the gap.

Insert them by making a hole in the stick with the bodkin and pushing the pointed end of the border stake into the hole (fig.5). Make sure that they are firmly in place. If not, make the holes bigger and try again.

☐ Starting towards the back put on a plait border all the way round the cradle, over the edge of the thick sticks, down the side of the gap and up the opposite side.

Handles

☐ Cut 2 pieces of 8mm (⁵⁄₁₆") handle cane, one 30.5cm (12") long and the other 51cm (20") long. Slype both ends of the longer piece and bend it into a U-shape with a flat bottom (fig.6).

☐ Remove the handle liners along the sides and insert the handle cane.

☐ Slype one end of the shorter piece of handle cane and bend the cane 15cm (6") from the pointed end (fig.7).

☐ Remove the handle liner at the back and insert the slyped end of the handle cane so that it is leaning towards the other handle cane.

☐ Cut a wedge into the forward end of the handle so that it fits snugly into the cane of the cross handle.

☐ Leave these handles in this position to dry.

☐ Stick the wedge-cut to the cross handle and nail through the cross handle so that the nail passes into the end of the other part of the handle (fig.8).

☐ Using No.6 (2.6mm) chair seating cane wrap the handle by starting at the back with the usual cross and leader. When you are 2.5cm (1") from the cross handle take the leader right over the top and round to the underside. Continue wrapping so that the end of the leader is also bound in. Peg the end of the wrapping cane, which will be bound in later.

☐ Wrap the cross handle in the usual way, using a leader as before. When you reach the centre bind in the wrapping cane from the other part of the handle. Criss-cross the wrapping over at this point so that the handle cane is completely covered. Keep the pattern of the leader the same as for the other side and finish off.

☐ Peg all three ends of the handle just under the waling.

Square work:needlecase and magazine cover

Square work is the most difficult regular-shaped basketry to do. It is worked very differently from other shapes which have some sticks threaded through others to start the base. To start square work the base is not made with a criss-cross pattern of sticks as in round or oval work.

The terms square work or square basketry are used loosely as they denote baskets which have corners and are usually rectangular—very few baskets are ever really square.

Flat square work

To begin square basketry start practising by making flat bases. Two small square 'mats' will make a needlecase or a notebook cover. With more experience you can make binder covers for recipes and magazines, a cover for a scrapbook or use six square bases as

a set of place mats. Working on a larger scale you can make window shutters and a headboard for a bed as shown in the next chapter.

Screwblock

A screwblock is used to start square work. Screwblocks can be bought from crafts stores but these tend to be very light and small and only suitable for very light work. It is easy to make one at home and also inexpensive.

The width of a square base is limited to the length of the screwblock. Normally 38cm (15″) is adequate but for larger items—for example a headboard—you would need a screwblock 66cm (26″) long.

You will need:

2 softwood strips 50mm x 75mm (2″x3″), 38cm (15″) long (or, for a larger screw-

Below: the completed binder cover, showing the attractive whipped borders.

Above: opened binder showing detail of the rings used to assemble covers.

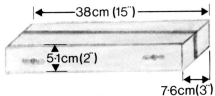

1. *Making a screwblock.*

2. *The thick outer sticks are trimmed to the same thickness as the cane used for the inner sticks.*

block, 2 pieces of softwood 75mm x 75mm (3″x3″), 66cm (26″) long).

Two 15cm (6″) coach bolts with a diameter of 6mm (¼″). Wing nuts and washers to fit the bolt. These are suitable for both screwblocks.

Hand drill and bit large enough to drill holes for the coach bolts.

☐ Place the two pieces of wood together as shown in fig.1, and drill two holes 7.5cm (3″) from each end. The holes are drilled through two pieces to make sure that the holes correspond.

☐ Push the bolts through the holes and screw on the washers and wing nuts.

Using the screwblock

To start a base the stakes are placed upright between the two parts of the screwblock. The wing nuts are then tightened to secure the stakes.

The base sticks are cut to the length required plus 2.5cm-5cm (1″-2″) for clamping in the screwblock plus enough to trim the ends once the work is complete.

The size of the cane used, the number of base sticks and the distance between the sticks will vary according to the size and function of the finished article. Generally the sticks on each edge are thicker than those inside so that the edges are neat and firm. Sometimes these outer sticks are doubled to give a really strong base.

If the outer sticks are thicker than the inner ones they won't fit into the screwblock without some preparation. The thicker sticks need to be cut down so that the part that is clamped in the screwblock is the same thickness as the smaller sticks. Make two cuts about 2.5cm (1″) from the end of each of the thicker sticks (fig.2). Try to make the cuts as square as possible and not tapered. The sticks are now ready for the screwblock.

Remember that the larger the article

the thicker the cane must be and the number of sticks must also be increased. The distance between the sticks will determine the distance between the side stakes later, so don't have them too far apart. For small items place the sticks 12mm-19mm (½″-¾″) apart and for medium-sized items 25mm-31mm (1″-1¼″) apart.

Needlecase

The cover consists of two bases each measuring about 8.5cm x 12.5cm (3¼″x 5″) and could equally well be used to cover a notebook.

This will give you the necessary experience to embark on a larger project.

As the materials used are small in quantity, there is little waste if the results are not entirely satisfactory.

You will need:

28gm (1oz) No.3 (2mm) cane.
142cm (56″) No.6 (2.6mm) cane.
71cm (28″) No.12 (3.75mm) cane.
4 small panel pins.
2 binder rings 18mm (¾″) diameter—available from stationers.
Felt to fit inside cover.
No.2 (1.85mm) chair seating cane 1.83m (2yd) long, or narrow enamelled wrapping cane—optional.
Tools as used for previous chapters and a screwblock.

☐ Cut 2 sticks of No.12 (3.75mm) cane and 4 sticks of No.6 (2.6mm) cane—all 18cm (7″) long.

☐ Trim one end of each of the thick sticks (fig.2).

☐ Place these two sticks in the screwblock 7.5cm (3″) apart—measure from the centre of one stick to the centre of the other.

☐ Place the 4 thinner sticks between the 2 sticks in the screwblock. Space them evenly and keep them upright.

☐ Tighten the screwblock so that all the sticks are held firmly in position. You may have cut the outer ones too much or too little so that they, or the inner ones, wobble about. If so, adjust them or cut new ones—you cannot make a good base unless all the sticks are firmly held.

Although a square base is mainly randed, the first row is paired and the last row is mock paired.

☐ Take a length of No.3 (2mm) cane and loop it round the left hand outer stick so that you have a long end and a short end of 20cm (8″). Use these 2 weavers and pair to the other end (fig.3).

☐ Drop the short end and continue with the long end only. Take it round the right-hand outer stick and then rand back to the left. Continue to rand backwards and forwards but on every other round the weaver must be taken round the outside sticks twice. This is because as you rand backwards and

The borders of the needlecase are whipped with enamelled wrapping cane to secure them to the base. Binder rings are used to assemble the needlecase with a piece of felt between the covers. Designer Barbara Maynard.

forwards you pass twice over the centre sticks while going round each outer stick once only. The extra twist will prevent any grins (gaps) appearing along the thick sticks (fig.4). If the randing is packed down you will need less double twists—adjust the wraps round the outer sticks as you work to cover the sticks but try to be constant, ie an extra wrap on every second or third round.

☐ Measure the width of the work as you go along to make sure that the canes do not slope inwards or outwards. It is very important when doing square work to see that the sticks remain upright and parallel. Measure as you progress and don't let the sticks lean backwards or forwards.

Joining new weavers is done exactly as for round and oval work. Make sure that the ends always lie at the back of the work which will become the wrong side.

☐ Continue randing until the work measures 11.5cm (4½″) in height. There should still be a short length of the sticks showing beyond the randing. This is for the last row which is mock pairing.

Mock pairing

☐ End the randing so that the weaver is on the left side of the work and has passed round the outer stick.

☐ Mock pair by taking the weaver in front of one stick and behind one stick, but each time it comes to the front, thread it underneath the weaver of the previous row. It should look just like pairing (fig.5).

☐ Continue all the way across to the end until the weaver reaches the right hand outer stick. Remove the work from the screwblock and trim all the weaver ends but do not cut any of the surplus stick ends yet.

☐ Replace the work in the screwblock and tighten it. This is to put on the first border.

3-rod border for square work

Cut 6 border stakes 12.5cm (5″) long and one piece 20cm (8″) long, all from No.3 (2mm) cane.

Trim the surplus stick ends of the inner sticks only and place the screwblock and work so that the wrong side of the work faces you.

☐ Insert one border stake into the weaving beside and to the left of each of the inner sticks. In this case (because the work is so small) insert the stakes about 2.5cm (1″) into the weaving.

☐ Insert one border stake down the side of the left outer stick.

☐ Using a bodkin to help you, insert one border stake into the weaving in front of the left outer stick and bend this down to the front of the work.

☐ Loop the 20cm (8″) border stake in the middle and wrap it round the outer left hand stick and the border stake next to it (fig.6). You should now have 3 stakes to the front and 5 still standing upright.

The 3 stakes to the front represent the first 3 stakes that are bent down to start a normal 3-rod border.

☐ Take stake 1 and pass it in front of the outer stick and stake 3 and behind stake 5 and back to the front (fig.7). Bend stake 3 down to lie behind and

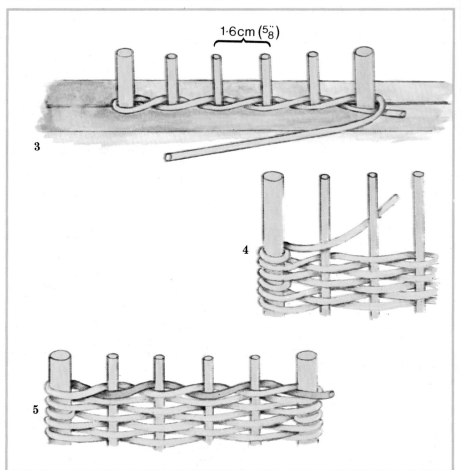

3. *Start needlecase cover with one row of pairing.*
4. *Extra twists on the outer sticks prevent gaps showing.*
5. *Mock pairing completes the base weaving.*

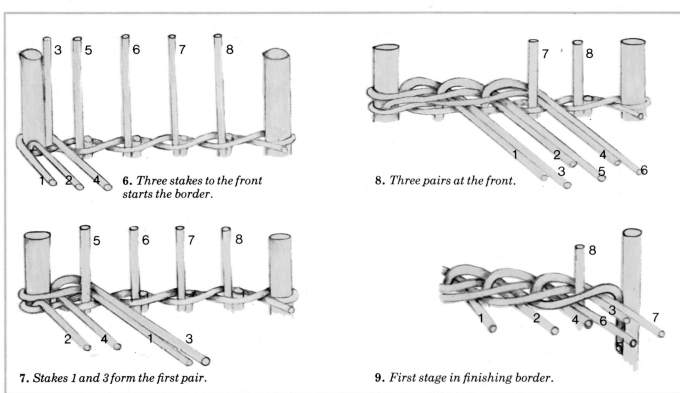

6. *Three stakes to the front starts the border.*

8. *Three pairs at the front.*

7. *Stakes 1 and 3 form the first pair.*

9. *First stage in finishing border.*

beside stake 1.

□ Take stake 2 in front of stake 5 and behind stake 6 and back to the front.

□ Bend stake 5 to lie behind and beside stake 2.

□ Take stake 4 in front of stake 6 and behind stake 7 and back to the front.

□ Bend stake 6 down to lie behind and beside stake 4. You will now have 3 pairs to the front (fig.8).

On a larger edge you would continue with a 3-rod border in the usual way but for this small base there is room for only one more stake.

□ Take the fifth stake from the right in front of stake 7 and behind stake 8 and back to the front.

□ Bend down stake 7 from last pair.

Finishing the 3-rod border

□ Take stake 3, the longer of the pair, in front of stake 8 and up to the right hand outer stick.

□ Nip this border stake so that it will bend down just before the outer stick. Cut it off about 3.5cm (1½″) below the nip and point the end. Push the pointed end into the weaving beside the outer stick (fig.9).

□ Bend down stake 8 (the last one) and pass it behind and right round the outer stick and thread it under the bent down stake (the last one you used) from the front to the back (fig.10).

This stake can be left there so trim it neatly or it can be threaded through the work once more so that it lies on the same side as all the other ends—which is the back of the work.

□ Secure the border by hammering a small panel pin into the border stakes that went round the two outer sticks,

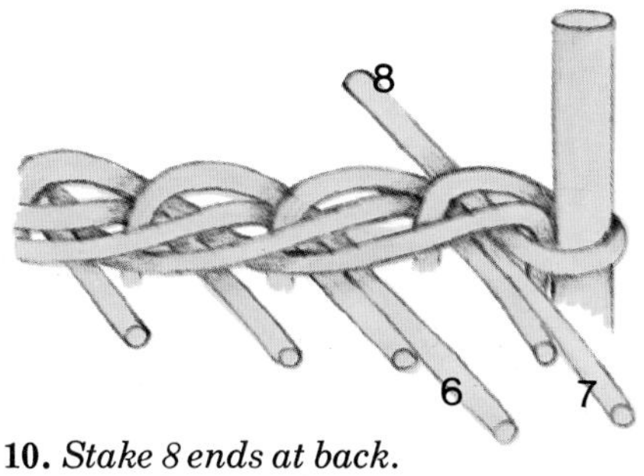

and into the outer sticks (fig.11).

□ Put on the same 3-rod border on the other edge. Start with the wrong side of the work facing you.

□ Cut off the protruding outer sticks close to the border and trim off surplus border stake ends.

Whipping

The border can be secured further by binding it in one or two places with fine chair seating cane. This is known as whipping.

□ Insert the cane into the weaving about 18mm (¾″) down from the border between two stakes. Use the long end to bind over the border and back through the randing at the same place 7 or 8 times. Wrap the short end in as you work. Try to make the whipping fan out over the border but keep it in the same place in the randing.

□ Secure the end by looping it once or twice through the whipping at the back and then weave it away.

□ Work another base in exactly the same way for the other cover taking great care to keep them both the same size.

□ Put 2 binder rings through the weaving on one side of the covers and cut felt to fit. Make holes to coincide with the rings and insert between covers to complete.

Magazine cover

Two bases measuring 23cm x 33cm (9″x13″) are joined with two binder rings to form the cover.

You will need:

170gm (6oz) No.6 (2.6mm) cane.
No.15 (4.5mm) cane 3.66m (4yd) long.
10mm handle cane 1.83m (2yd) long.
4 small panel pins.
3 binder rings.
No.4 (2.25mm) chair seating cane or wrapping cane 3.66m (4yd) long—optional.

□ Cut 2 sticks of 10mm handle cane 38cm (15″) long, and 6 sticks of No.15 (4.5mm) cane 38cm (15″) long.

□ Cut one end of each of the 2 thick sticks to fit into the screwblock with the other sticks.

□ Arrange the sticks in the screwblock so that the 2 outer ones—centre to centre—are 23cm (9″) apart and space the inner sticks evenly.

□ Using No. 6 (2.6mm) cane put on one row of pairing.

□ Rand for 31cm (12¼″) and put on one row of mock pairing.

□ Using No.6 (2.6mm) cane border down as for the previous cover. You will need 9 stakes 20cm (8″) long and one to loop round the outer stick 38cm (15″) long.

□ Pin the border down with panel pins and whip with chair seating cane if you wish.

□ Repeat the above to make the second cover. Insert binder rings to complete.

10. *Stake 8 ends at back.*

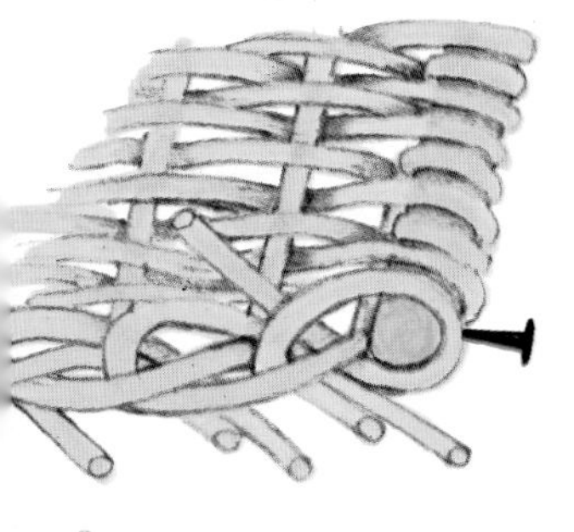

11. *Nail secures border to outer thick stick.*

Square work patterns: cover and headboard

One of the interesting things about doing square work is that patterns can be incorporated into the designs. The patterns given here can be varied depending on the size of the piece you are making.

The plain magazine cover given in the previous project should be a comfortable size to work on, and helps you to become familiar with patterns.

Cover with pattern

Make the cover as described in the previous project, setting the sticks up in the screwblock, pair and then rand until the work measures 12.5cm (5″) and the weaver has passed in the front of the centre stick.

For working the pattern you will find that you need extra twists round the outer sticks.

☐ On the next row the weaver must once again pass in front of the centre stick. To do this the weaver must pass behind 2 sticks instead of only one on either side of the centre stick.

☐ The next row will be normal and then the odd row must be repeated. Add one more normal row.

This completes one stage of the pattern. There are five stages consisting of 5 rows each. On the next two stages the pattern is extended and the two after that are decreased to form the diamond shape illustrated.

☐ For the next stage the same thing is done but the weaver must pass in front of the two sticks on either side of the centre stick five times. This is achieved by passing behind the 2 successive sticks next to the centre stick instead of one on every alternate row. Five rows complete the second stage.

☐ The weaver must now go in front of

the centre stick and the second stick on either side of it for 5 rows. Pass behind 2 sticks on every alternate row for 5 rows.

☐ Repeat the first and the second stage in reverse order to complete the pattern.

☐ Continue randing as before to finish. Add a row of mock pairing and put on a border.

The headboard

The headboard is 91.5cm (1yd) wide and 51cm (20″) high. It can be used to replace an existing headboard or you can attach it to the wall by hooks secured to the wall with wall plugs and positioned to hook round the sticks where the coil pattern starts.

Working with such thick sticks can be awkward so do not attempt it until you have some experience with square work.

You will need:
677gm (1½lb) No.8 (3mm) cane.
No.15 (4.5mm) cane, 5.5m (6yd) long.
9 lengths of 8mm handle cane, 102cm (40″) long or 9 lengths of dowelling—6mm (¼″) diameter—102cm (40″) long.
2 lengths of dowelling—18mm (¾″) diameter—102cm (40″) long.
12 small panel pins.
Screwblock—at least 66cm (26″) long.
Adhesive tape.

☐ Cut the 2 thick sticks so that the ends fit into the screwblock with the 9 inner sticks.

☐ Place the thick sticks so that they are 48cm (19″) apart—centre to centre —and space the other sticks evenly between them.

☐ Weave with well-soaked No.8 (3mm) cane starting with one row of pairing and continue to rand backwards and

The cover with pattern (detail below) can be used as a scrapbook or for recipes. Designer: Barbara Maynard.

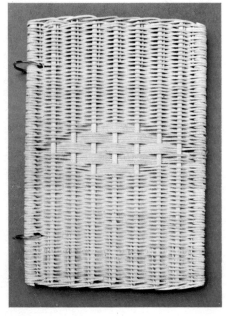

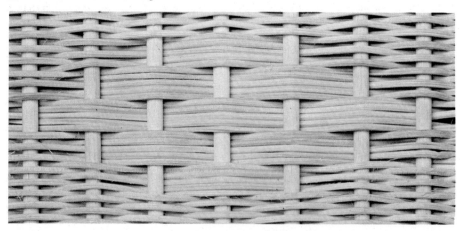

forwards for 16.5cm (6½").

☐ Cut the third inner stick from the left level with the randing. Insert one length of No.15 (4.5mm) cane (it must be at least 2.74m (3yd) long) into the weaving just to the left of the fourth inner stick from the left. Coil this piece round and round for about 58cm (22") and secure it with adhesive tape against the 2 sticks. Leave enough space after the last coil to allow you to put on 16.5cm (6½") of randing and a row of mock pairing.

☐ Rand backwards and forwards on the first 3 sticks on the left only for 61cm (2') catching in the coil when convenient.

☐ Cut the third inner stick from the right and place a length of No.15 (4.5mm) cane against the second inner stake from the right. Repeat the coiling as before and end it 7.5cm (3") short of the previous coils.

☐ Rand backwards and forwards on the 3 inner sticks and then on the 3 right-hand sticks, catching in the coils as you work. Rand to the end of the second length of coil.

☐ You now have to replace the cut stick. Measure the length you need from the end of the coil to the end of the

other sticks and add on an additional piece before cutting. Use adhesive tape to keep it in position against the coils until there is enough randing to hold it securely. Remove adhesive tape and pull the stick up so that the end is butting up to the last coil.

☐ Rand backwards and forwards to the first coil and catch it in where convenient. At the same time bind in the end of the coil cane.

☐ Replace the other missing stick in the same way and rand right across for a further 16.5cm (6½").

☐ Finish with one row of mock pairing.

☐ The border is put on in the same way as before but insert one stake on each side of each stick otherwise the border will be too loose. You will therefore need 20 stakes 25.5cm (10") long and one longer piece 50.5cm (20") long all of No.8 (3mm) cane, for each end.

☐ Try to keep these border stakes inserted to the same depth all the way along. Nip them down and put the border on as before.

☐ Nail the four panel pins into the corners and put in a nail through the end of each coil into the adjoining stick to keep the coils steady.

Headboard made on a large screwblock with coil pattern (detail below).

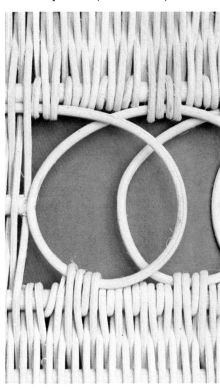

Bottle tote and picnic hamper

When you have mastered the technique of flat square work so that you feel confident, you can then progress and build up square baskets. Square baskets are suitable for sewing boxes, picnic hampers and wine baskets, etc. The instructions in this chapter make it possible for you to combine tech- niques and designs so that you can adapt the baskets to your own needs.

The techniques include upsetting, fastenings, hinges, small handles and rib randing. The techniques used for making the lid and hinges are suitable for other shapes such as oval and round work, and the small handles can be put

on to any basket where you do not require a large handle.

Bottle tote

Start with this basket as it is easier than the basket with the lid. The basket measures 20cm x 30cm (8"x 11¾"), and is 20cm (8") high excluding the handle. The basket is big and strong enough to hold six bottles.

You will need:
57gm (2oz) No.5 (2.5mm) cane.
170gm (6oz) No.6 (2.6mm) cane.
113gm (4oz) No.10 (3.35mm) cane.
No.15 (4.5mm) cane, 1.83m (6') long.
No.8 (3mm) cane, 2.44m (8') long.
10mm handle cane, 91.5cm (3') long—

use Malacca cane if you can obtain it.
8mm handle cane, 2.14m (7') long.
2 handle liners.
Screwblock and usual tools.

For the base cut the 8mm handle cane into 7 pieces, each 30.5cm (12") long. Split three of these right down the centre along the length. They will split easily if you make a small cut with a trimming knife, and then pull them apart with your fingers. Five of the split handle canes will form the inner sticks of the base—the sixth piece is discarded.

☐ Set the sticks up in the screwblock with double whole canes on the outsides. The distance between the outer sticks must be 18cm (7")—centre to centre. Trim the outer sticks to fit into the block with inner sticks. Set the split canes up so that they are evenly spaced between the outer sticks. Let the curved side of the split canes face you.

☐ Weaving with No.5 (2.5mm) cane put on one row of pairing, then rand and finish off with one row of mock pairing so that the base is 27cm (10½") high. Remember to twist the weaver around the outer stick on every second or third round to avoid grins (gaps) showing. Keep the sticks upright and do not let the work get wider or narrower towards the top.

☐ Remove the base from the screwblock and trim the ends of the weavers and the four ends of the outer sticks—*do not trim the inner sticks for the time being.*

For the stake up cut 21 stakes 46cm (18") long and 14 stakes 51cm (20") long, all from No.10 (3.35mm) cane. Point the 21 shorter ones at one end with a short point and the others with the usual longer point.

☐ Place the base flat on the table with the trimmed ends upwards. This will become the inside of the basket.

☐ Use the bodkin to form a channel and insert one of the longer stakes into the base between the outer sticks of one corner. It does not matter if the stake lies underneath the two sticks in the crevice that is formed by the roundness of the canes. Repeat with another stake at the other end along the length.

☐ Stake up along the length. Eleven of the shorter stakes must be inserted into one side along the length of the work. Use a pencil and make marks 6mm (¼") in from the corners. Make nine more marks, evenly spaced between the two outside marks.

☐ Use the bodkin to make holes through both the outer sticks in which to insert the stakes. Start at one end and insert each stake as you go along. Push the bodkin into the outer sticks from the outside and in between the weaving canes where the marks are. Make the holes quite large. Most diffi-

Two examples of square baskets: the picnic basket with a lid, and the bottle tote with partitions to separate bottles. Designer: Barbara Maynard.

1 Diagonal cuts
to fit against
each other

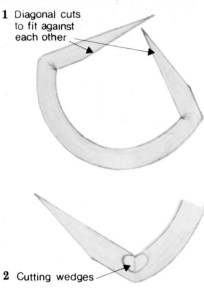

2 Cutting wedges

Top: well-soaked canes are twisted to form the partitions for the bottles.

1. *Diagonals cut to fit each other.*
2. *Wedges cut in cane before bending.*

culties encountered in staking up square work are caused by holes which are not large enough. Pull the bodkin out and insert the stake immediately. The hole closes up quickly when the bodkin is removed, so if you were not quick enough open the hole again with the bodkin and try again.

Insert the stake until you can see the point on the inside of the outer sticks. Make sure that all the pointed section is inside the sticks—if it is not the stake will crack and split on the upsett.

☐ Now repeat on the opposite side. Insert 2 long stakes between the outer sticks (as before). Instead of eleven stakes along the length, 10 stakes are inserted to create an odd number which makes randing easier.

☐ Cut off any surplus ends from the inner sticks and insert one of the long stakes beside each stick at each end. It doesn't matter which side of the stick they are inserted but try to space them evenly.

For the upsett make sure that the stakes are well soaked and nip each one close to the base. Bend them all up together and tie tightly. If you have not trimmed all the outer base sticks, do so now.

☐ Insert 4 weavers of No.6 (2.6mm) cane into the base and 4-rod wale for one round. Continue with a 3-rod wale for 4 rounds. Keep the corner stakes close together and do not try to space them evenly—the closer together they are, the squarer the corners will be. Keep the waling upright.

☐ Cut 8 bye-stakes 20.5cm (8″) long, of No.15 (4.5mm) cane. Point one end of each and insert them into the waling—insert 2 bye-stakes at each corner, next to a stake on the side closest to the corner.

The thicker bye-stakes are used to make the corners stronger and also help to keep the corners square.

☐ Cut 27 bye-stakes 20.5cm (8″) long, of No.10 (3.35mm) cane and insert them into the waling beside and to the right of the remaining stakes.

☐ Rand with No.6 (2.6mm) cane keeping the work straight up and the corners as square as possible. Continue until the randing measures 7cm (2¾″).

☐ Put on 3 rounds of waling using No.6 (2.6mm) cane.

☐ Insert the handle liners in the centre of the two short sides.

Rib randing is a decorative variation of randing. It is done by passing the cane in front of two stakes and behind one (instead of in front of one and behind one). This makes a thicker weave with a slight spiral effect. You have to have a number of stakes that will not divide by 3 or the weaver will go in front of the same stakes each time.

☐ Rib rand for 5cm (2″) with No.6 (2.6mm) cane.

☐ Wale with No.6 (2.6mm) cane for 3 rounds.

For the partitions cut a piece of well soaked No.8 (3mm) cane twice the width of the basket plus 30.5cm (12″). Bend it in the middle and loop it over a stake one third of the way down along the length. Twist the two ends together, quite tightly, until the twisted length is sufficient to reach across to the other side. Loop the two ends around a corresponding stake on the other side, one end going round one way and the other, the other way round. Weave the ends away on top of the waling.

☐ Repeat with a second piece of cane two thirds of the way along the length so that there are three equal partitions.

☐ Cut a piece of No.8 (3mm) cane, twice the length of the basket, plus 30.5cm (12″). Bend it in the middle and loop it over one of the handle liners and its adjoining stake. Twist the ends together until it reaches the first of the cross partitions. Pass one cane around each side of the cross twist and continue to twist until you reach the next cross partition and pass the cane around it as before. Twist again until you reach the other end and finish as before.

☐ Trim the surplus ends of the bye-stakes, re-soak the stakes if necessary and nip them 6mm (¼″) above the waling.

☐ Put on a 4-rod border. Try to keep the corners very square. Trim all the surplus ends.

☐ Point each end of the 10mm handle cane and shape the handle into a flat U-shape. Remove the liners and insert the handle well down into the work.

☐ Cut 12 pieces of No.6 (2.6mm) cane, 1.2m (40″) long. Insert six to the left of each end of the handle. Rope the handle and finish with a herringbone pattern as described on page 25.

Picnic hamper with lid

The outside measurements of the hamper are 38cm x 25.5cm (15″x 10″), height 14cm (5½″). The lid is secured with hinges and fasteners.

You will need:
170gm (6oz) No.5 (2.5mm) cane.
170gm (6oz) No.6 (2.6mm) cane.
170gm (6oz) No.10 (3.35mm) cane.
113gm (4oz) No.15 (4.5mm) cane.
No.8 (3mm) cane, 2.74m (3yd) long.
No.4 (2mm) chair seating cane, 7.32m (8yd) long.
8mm handle cane, 4.57m (5yd) long.
4 small nails or panel pins.
All-purpose adhesive.
Screwblock and tools as for previous chapters.
Small D-shaped handle—make this first so that it is ready when the time comes to fix it on.

□ Cut a piece of 8mm handle cane 35.5cm (14″) long. Soak it well and bend it into a U-shape. Nip it hard with the round-nose pliers 10cm (4″) in from each end. These 10cm (4″) sections form the straight side of the handle and each piece must be shaved away with a diagonal cut so that they form one thickness when put together (fig.1). If the ends will not come round far enough cut out a wedge shape where you nipped the cane (fig.2).

□ Tie the handle together in its correct shape and leave to dry. Glue the ends together and again tie in position and leave to dry.

□ Wrap the handle with chair seating cane. Start at the back of the handle which is the straight side—start and finish as for the handle of the wine cradle, as described on page 32. The corners may be difficult to keep tidy-wrap tightly and just do your best. You may use a leader on the curved side and, if you join it in before the corners, it will help to cover the corners.

For the base cut four outer sticks of 8mm handle cane and 16 inner sticks (these are not split) of No.15 (4.5mm) cane—all 40.5cm (16″) long. Set them up in the screwblock with the handle cane on the outside and 23cm (9″) apart. Space the other sticks evenly.

□ Make the base as before—one row of pairing to start, then rand and finish with one row of mock pairing when the work measures 31cm (13½″)—all with No.5 (2.5mm) cane.

□ Using No.10 (3.35mm) cane, cut 27 stakes 35.5cm (14″) long, and 20 stakes 40.5cm (16″) long.

Stake up as before with the shorter stakes along the length and the long stakes into the ends.

□ Nip the stakes and tie them up into two bunches—one at each end. This will prevent the base from becoming distorted and curling up.

Upsett with one row of 4-rod waling and three rows of 3-rod waling with No.6 (2.6mm) cane.

□ Cut 39 bye-stakes of No.10 (3.35mm) and eight of No.15 (4.5mm) cane for the corners—all 12.5cm (5″) long. Insert them as before.

□ Rand for 5cm (2″) with No.6 (2.6mm) cane.

To fix the handle mark its position in the centre of the long side you prefer. Select two stakes, one at each end of the flat side of the handle, which are convenient to carry the loops that will secure the handle.

□ Cut 2 pieces of No.8 (3mm) cane, 35.5cm (14″) long. Make sure that they are well soaked and not brittle. Bend one in the middle and loop it round one of the selected stakes about 1.8cm (¾″) down from the top of the randing. Twist this cane for 1.8cm (¾″) by taking one end in each hand and crossing your

hands over. Transfer the canes into the other hands and repeat for the required length. This method produces a tight even twist.

□ Place the handle in position so that the twist comes through the inside of the handle. Take the two ends of the twist upwards and loop them round the back of the same stake over the top of the randing. Weave the two ends away. Do not make the twist too loose nor too tight. If it is loose the handle will have too much play and if it is tight it will chafe the loops.

□ Repeat with another loop at the other end of the handle.

□ Rand with No.6 (2.6mm) cane right round the basket. Continue until the randing measures 7.5cm (3″).

□ Wale with No.6 (2.6mm) cane for four rounds.

□ Put on a 3-rod border and a follow-on trac border.

The lid. If you have made your basket absolutely perfect the lid will be exactly the same shape as the base and slightly larger to allow for the upsett. However, as the shape is never constant, the lid must be made to fit the shape at the top of the basket.

A template is made by turning the basket upside down and placing it on a sheet of card. Draw all the way round the basket. This is to be the shape of the lid. Cut the template out to enable you to follow it closely (fig.3).

3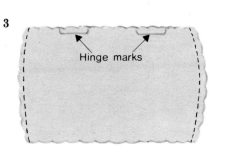

3. *Template for lid with hinge marks.*

□ Mark the position of the hinges on the template along the length on the side opposite the handle.

□ Cut 6mm (¼″) from the short sides of the template to allow for the borders.

□ Cut four sticks of 8mm handle cane and 16 of No.15 (4.5mm) cane—all the length of the template plus 5cm (2″). The extra 5cm (2″) is to allow for 2.5cm (1″) which goes into the screwblock and 2.5cm (1″) at the top end to make finishing easier.

□ Mark the outer stick along the side where the hinges are to be. Don't forget to allow for the extra length of the sticks.

□ At the hinge marks cut halfway through the thickness of the cane so that the cuts are 1.8cm (¾″) long (fig.4).

Detail of D-shaped handle, and the hasp and loop for securing lid.

□ Set the sticks in the screwblock to fit the template with the hinge cuts positioned as illustrated. Allow for the thickness of the weaving cane on each side.

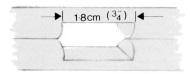

1·8cm ($\frac{3}{4}$)

4. Recesses cut to allow for hinges.

□ A stick with the hinge recesses must be on the inside with the recesses of both sticks matching (fig.5). Check that the sticks match up with the template.

□ Using No.5 (2.5mm) cane put on a row of pairing then, if the corners of the template are rounded, lift the pairing up to match the template. Place pieces of cane below the pairing to keep it in position (fig.5).

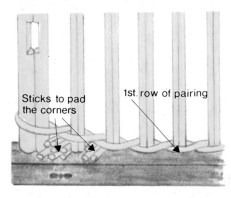

Sticks to pad the corners

1st. row of pairing

5. Sticks inserted to position pairing.

□ Using No.6 (2.6mm) cane continue randing but fill up the hollow between the corners by weaving backwards and forwards as shown on pages 27 and 28, until the weaving is straight all the way across. Continue randing and do not forget to pass the weaver twice around the outer stick on every second or third round, until you reach the first hinge mark.

□ Continue to rand backwards and forwards but pass the cane round the inner of the two outside sticks so that the weaver settles into the cut-away part. When the end of the hinge mark is reached revert back to passing right round the outer sticks.

□ Follow the template to the other hinge and repeat the method of making the hinge space. Continue to the end of the lid. Pack again (weaving backwards and forwards going to one stake less each time) if necessary to make the rounded shape of the template.

□ Finish with one row right across and put on one row of mock pairing.

□ Complete the lid with a 3-rod border at each end and whip the borders with chair seating cane. Secure the border with small nails or panel pins.

The hinges on baskets are very simple.

□ Take a length of No.5 (2.5mm) cane (or chair seating cane) and insert it into the basket just under the border. Leave 23cm (9″) free on the inside (which will be woven away). Take the long end up and over the outer stick of the lid, through the hinge recess, down inside the lid and basket and back to the outside of the basket under the border so that it lies side by side with the other end. Continue doing this, over and over, until the hinge recess is filled up.

□ Weave both ends away in the waling of the basket.

□ Repeat with the other hinge.

Fastenings—make two loops in the front of the basket, using No.8 (3mm) cane, in exactly the same way as for the loops that hold the handle. Select two suitable stakes, about 7.5cm (3″) in from each end. Start the loops about 18mm ($\frac{3}{4}$″) down from the waling and finish them just underneath the waling.

The hasps are similar or they may be plaited instead. These are started and finished in the lid and drop down over the front and round the loops.

□ Loop a piece of No.8 (3mm) cane round the first inner sticks from the front edge of the lid, and slightly to the left side of the loop in the basket.

□ Add a third cane for a plait. Twist (or plait) until there is sufficient length to go right round the loop on the opposite side from which you started and back up to meet the twist (or plait) again (fig.6). Here it crosses over

6. Cane twisted to form the hasp.

itself—take one end of the canes through the twist (or plait)—and continue until you reach the first inner stick again, this time slightly to the right. Weave the ends away and repeat on the other side.

□ Fasten the basket with a stick made from handle cane. Cut a piece long enough to pass through both loops with 5cm (2″) to overlap at both ends. Point one end.

The other end may be left plain or make a loop of No.15 (1.5mm) cane, shaped and glued in place, and then wrapped over with chair seating cane.

Basketry lampshades

Basketry lampshades give a warm, attractive light and seem to suit most types of houses and cottages, but they are expensive to buy. However they are quite easy and inexpensive to make as they use very little cane.

This type of lampshade is open at both ends so the stakes are initially held in position in holes made in a cardboard disc. A wire ring with a bulb fitting must be inserted in the lampshade. In other words the lampshade is made to measure after a suitable lampshade ring has been selected. The rings are available in a wide range of sizes and shapes and are suitable for all types of light fittings.

Cylindrical shade

Start with a cylindrical shade, ie straight-sided with a circular cross-section with the same diameter throughout. The shade illustrated was made on a 23cm (9″) ring with a flat fitting and is 20cm (8″) high.

You will need:
Tools—as for previous chapters.
Thick cardboard disc with 30.5cm (12″) diameter.
23cm (9″) diameter lampshade ring.
Lampshade tape—enough to cover the ring.
56gm (2oz) No.6 (2.6mm) cane.
28gm (1oz) No.5 (2.5mm) cane.
56gm (2oz) flat cane—this is similar to the ordinary cane except that it is flat and only available in one size.
Needle and cotton to secure ring in position.

☐ Place the lampshade ring on the cardboard and draw round it with pencil. Mark the pencil ring at approximately 25mm (1″) intervals all the way round. There should be about 29 marks but, whatever the number, make sure that it will not divide by three otherwise you will not be able to rib rand as you have been shown on page 44. If necessary, alter the number of marks to adjust this.

☐ Bind the lampshade ring with the tape so that it is ready to insert later.

☐ Pierce the cardboard with the bodkin at each of the marks just outside the pencilled ring. The holes should be just big enough to take the No.6 (2.6mm) cane. If the holes are too big the stakes will slip about too easily and will make the first process difficult.

☐ Cut one stake for each of the holes from No.6 (2.6mm) cane, 61cm (24″) long.

☐ Insert one stake into each hole and pull them through so that 20cm (8″) protrudes on one side for the first border. Nip the short ends near the cardboard so that they turn down easily without cracking.

☐ The next step is putting on a border which will form either the top or bottom of the shade. If you put this border on in the usual way, ie from left to right, you will find that when you turn it up the other way to start the weaving, the stakes will lean over to the right which makes it difficult to control them. This is avoided by putting down the border going the other way, ie from right to left.

Put on a 3-rod border (fig.1) working from right to left. You will find it easier if you rest the edge of the cardboard disc on a table with the long ends pointing towards you. Stand up and lean over the cardboard to manipulate the border canes. Do not trim the ends when finished.

☐ When the border is complete turn the shade so that the cardboard is flat on the table. Place a weight inside the cardboard to keep it steady.

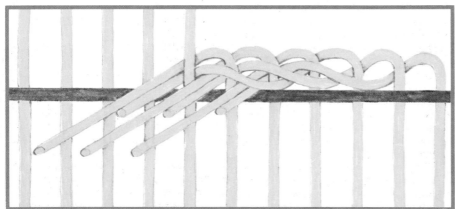

Left: the shade is started with a 3-rod border, working from right to left.

☐ Using No.5 (2.5mm) cane put on 5 rounds of waling. Remember to step-up at the end of each round.

☐ Cut 2 bye-stakes of No.6 (2.6mm) cane for each stake—all 20cm (8″) long. Point one end of each and insert them —one on each side of each stake—into the work.

☐ Rib rand (in front of two, behind one and back to the front) with flat cane for 14cm (5½″). Be very careful to keep the sides quite straight.

☐ Wale with No.5 (2.5mm) cane for one round and insert the taped ring, which should fit exactly, then continue with 4 more rows of waling.

If you let the sides curve in or out and the ring will not fit, insert it from the other end.

☐ Nip the *stakes* 6mm (¼″) above the waling and cut off all the surplus ends of the *bye-stakes*.

☐ Put on a 3-rod border in the normal way (left to right) and a follow-on trac border.

☐ Turn the shade the other way up to finish the first border.

If you are making a number of shades and want to re-use the cardboard disc, undo the border and gently pull the cardboard up and away from the stakes. Set the disc aside to dry. Turn the border down again (re-soak the stakes if necessary) and put on a follow-on trac border. Trim the ends.

If you are making one shade only and do not need to re-use the cardboard disc, soak it in water to soften it and then pull it away from the shade. Put on a follow-on trac border and trim.

☐ Stitch the ring in place to hold it securely. Do not stitch through the canes. Take the thread round the stakes only so that it is lost to sight between the waling.

Vase-shaped shade

The size of the shade is a matter of choice. The one illustrated was made with a 10cm (4″) lampshade ring and is 23cm (9″) high.

You will need:

Thick cardboard disc with 15cm (6″) diameter.

10cm (4″) diameter lampshade ring covered with tape.

56gm (2oz) No.6 (2.6mm) cane.

56gm (2oz) No.4 (2.25mm) cane.

Lampshades can be made in a variety of shapes. This vase-shaped shade incorporates double randing. The shade is mounted on to a lamp fitting without the usual base. It can be used on a base or as a hanging shade.

Needle and cotton to secure ring in position.

Lampshades are always started in the same way. The shape of the shade will affect the distance between the stakes depending on how much it curves outwards. If you want the shade to come out a great deal, the stakes round the ring will need to be much closer at the ring end so that they are not too far apart at the edge. Start this shade with the stakes 1.5cm ($\frac{5}{8}''$) apart to allow for the flow in the middle.

23 stakes were used for the lampshade illustrated. If you wish to rib rand, the number of stakes must not be divisible by three. To work a double rand any odd number is sufficient.

☐ Cut the stakes 61cm (24″) long using No.6 (2.6mm) cane. Insert them into the cardboard disc and put on a border as for the previous lampshade.

☐ Put on 4 rounds of waling with No.4 (2.25mm) cane.

☐ Using No.6 (2.6mm) cane cut one bye-stake for each stake. Point one end of each and insert the pointed ends into the waling to the right of the stakes.

☐ Double rand with 2 weavers of No.4 (2.25mm) cane. Always keep one weaver on top of the other and do not let them twist round. Support the stakes with the thumb and forefinger of the left hand. Try not to let the weavers dominate the stakes. Keep the sides of the stakes quite straight for 5cm (2″) then allow them to flow out to a diameter of 14cm (5½″). Try to make a 'bulb' shape. Decrease the diameter as you proceed to 10cm (4″).

☐ Put on 3 rounds of waling with No.4 (2.25mm) cane. Trim the bye-stakes and border down with a 3-rod border and follow-on trac border.

☐ Remove the cardboard and finish the first border as for cylindrical lampshade. Trim the weaver ends and stitch in the ring to finish.

Open-worked shade

This shade is not covered with weaving. The stakes are left open in parts and held in position with a row of fitching. The light bulb can be hidden by covering the inside of shade with a suitable lampshade lining material—available from large department stores.
The completed shade is 18cm (7″) high.
You will need:
9cm (3½″) diameter lampshade ring covered with tape.
Thick cardboard disc with 12.5cm (5″) diameter.
Thread, needle.
56gm (2oz) No.6 (2.6mm) cane.
28gm (1oz) No.4 (2.25mm) cane.
25cm (¼yd) lampshade lining material —optional.
☐ Make 21 holes round the pencilled ring on the cardboard as before.
☐ Cut 21 stakes 46cm (18″) long from

No.6 (2.6mm) cane and insert them into the holes in the cardboard disc so that 10cm (4″) protrude from one side.
☐ Put on a trac border—behind one, in front of three and tuck it to the inside in the next space—going from right to left.
☐ Turn the shade the other way up and put on 4 rounds of waling with No.4 (2.25mm) cane.
☐ Cut 42 bye-stakes of No.6 (2.6mm) cane 38cm (15″) long. Point them at one end and insert them into the waling— one on each side of each of the stakes.
☐ Nip these groups of 3 stakes so that they will bend outwards.
☐ Put on one round of fitching (the method is shown on page 14) 9cm (3½″) away from the waling to make the diameter of the shade 18cm (7″).
☐ Wale for 4 rounds with No.4 (2.25mm) cane and continue to shape the work outwards.
☐ Put on a trac border (left to right) with all three stakes in turn—behind one, in front of three and tuck the canes to the inside in the next space.
☐ Finish the first border as for the previous shades and trim all the ends.
☐ Shape and stitch lampshade lining material into the lampshade and stitch in the ring to finish.

Open-worked shades are quick to make and do not require much cane. The shade is worked from the smaller open end. The stakes and bye-stakes are bent outwards and held in position with a row of fitching. A trac border completes the shade. The shade has been coloured brown with a wood stain and lined with fabric to hide the light fitting.

Caning chair seats

With the help of simple basketry techniques, chairs with broken cane seats can be restored to their original strength and attractiveness. Chair caning is a fascinating traditional craft, and the results more than justify the time spent on it.

You will need:

a strong, sharp knife with a pointed blade

a clearer, for knocking out old plugs (such as a short, blunt metal rod)

a fine pointed bodkin, at least 7·6 cm (3″) long

a light hammer

about 6 wood or cane pegs, about 7·6 cm (3″) long and tapering to a point (golf tees are sometimes suitable)

227g (½lb) bundle of cane

1 length of No. 6 cane

The cane is the outer skin of the cane used in basketmaking, and it has a rough side and a smooth, shiny side. It is sold in 227g (½lb) bundles in sizes 1 to 6, but the size of cane and the amount used depends on the size and spacing of the holes and the pattern to be worked. For example, a small bedroom chair with 12 holes in a 15·2 cm (6″) length of rail would require 71 to 85g (2½ to 3oz) of cane for a standard 6-way pattern. If the holes are more closely spaced, a finer cane such as No. 2 could be used for the first stages with No. 3 for the diagonals.

To frame the finished seat, a beading of No. 5 or 6 or even glossy lapping cane, depending on the size of the holes, is laced down with No. 1 or 2. Alternatively, the beading can be omitted altogether if all the holes are plugged.

To cane a chair

The following instructions for a standard 6-way pattern apply only to a square or rectangular frame (flat, not dipped).

□ The chair needs to be cleared of the old seat. Turn it upside down, cut across all the strands between the holes, and carefully knock out all the plugs. These can be kept for replugging later. The seat can now be pushed out. It is possible to work the cane dry, but it is more pliable if it is damped and allowed to mellow. Choose the longest pieces of

Opposite: there is no need to throw out chairs with damaged cane seats. They can easily be repaired, and will look as good as new.

cane for the first stages.

First setting

The strands in the first setting run from the back to the front of the frame. Starting from the centre hole in the back rail, thread a piece of cane down so that half its length is underneath the chair.

□ Secure firmly, shiny side uppermost, either with a peg or by looping the lower end up through the frame and down the same hole, under the top end (fig. 1). Under tension, the top length bites on the loop and prevents it from slipping.

□ Thread top piece of cane down the centre hole of the front rail, pull tight and peg. Take it up through the next hole on the right of the centre front hole, over to the corresponding hole on the back rail, pull tight and peg (fig. 2).

□ Making sure the smooth side of the cane is always visible on top and under the frame, continue in this way until the hole before the corner. Then return to the end left in the centre of the chair and work the other half.

Joining the cane There are several ways in which cane can be joined. If the cane size is not much smaller than the size of the holes, put the old end down one hole and a loop of new cane down the next hole.

□ Thread the old end through the loop, and pull the loop up to the lower level of the hole (fig. 3).

□ The old end is taken down one hole, pegged and brought up into the next hole. Put the new end down into the second hole, hitch it under the old cane and back under itself, where it will hold under tension (fig. 4).

If there is already a strand between two holes, a new end may be wrapped twice round the existing strand.

First weaving The first weaving places the strands across from side to side of the frame.

□ Take the end of a cane across the underside of the corner and come up in the first hole on the side rail next to the corner hole. Lay the strand over the first settings to the corresponding hole on the opposite rail, and work from side to side until all the holes are used except those at the corners.

Second setting Using the same holes as the first setting, lay a second setting slightly to the left of the first one, positioning it over all the weavings (fig. 5). Make sure that on the underside the new strands fill the gaps between those already in position.

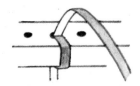
1

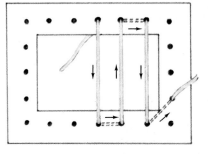
2

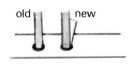
3

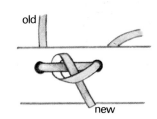
4

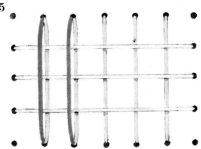
5

1. *Beginning the caning.*
2. *The first setting is worked from the back to the front of the frame.*
3. *The cane is joined by looping it over the old one.*
4. *Joining the cane by making a loop in the new end.*
5. *The second setting lies slightly to the left of the first one.*

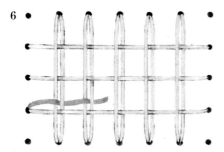

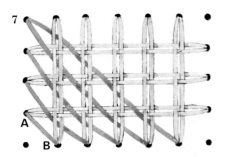

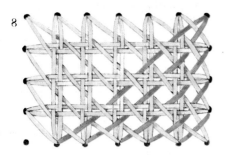

6. *The second weaving lies over the second setting and under the first.*
7. *The first diagonals lie in a south-east to north-west direction.*
8. *The second diagonals lie in the opposite direction to the first diagonals.*

Second weaving This is the first stage which is actually woven. It uses the same holes as the first weaving but the cane is woven over the second setting, under the first setting, and lies further away from the front rail than the first weaving from the same holes (fig. 6). It is easier to work this stage with just the last few inches of cane, pulling the whole length through only once or twice in the row.

☐ Work with one hand above and one below the frame, or use the point of a shell bodkin woven under three or four strands to guide the end of the cane through. As soon as a row is completed, draw it and the previous row down into position, or the second weaving will tend to curve upwards.

The first diagonals lie in a south-east to north-west direction. They always lie under the settings and over the weavings so that they slide easily into the corner of each junction and lie in a straight line. Once the basic weave is established, the main points to watch are the beginning and end of each row, to keep the edges of the chair tidy.

☐ Although the diagonals finish as a straight line, the process of working is like going up a series of steps. Apart from the line AB and the corresponding line in the opposite corner, all the diagonals must start and finish by using the projecting tips of the settings and weavings, passing under the setting tips and over the weaving tips (fig. 7). This means that each line is woven to the fullest extent and covers the wooden edge with a close, even texture of cane work.

☐ Two settings or weavings coming from the same hole are treated as one from this point onwards. Beginning again at the front near the bottom left-hand corner and using much shorter lengths of cane, work from one hole, under the setting tip on the left, up over the weaving, under the setting on the left and so on, ending up by working over the tip of the weaving and down the next hole above it. The diagonals can be worked backwards and forwards for a few rows at a time, but it is not necessary to join the ends.

Notice that two diagonals converge – called a 'double' – into the top left corner and into the bottom right corner (not the same two unless the frame is square). The bottom left and top right corners are missed out. When the second group of diagonals is worked the opposite holes will be doubled and missed so that the finished seat has two diagonals in every hole.

Second diagonals do the exact opposite to the first diagonals, going over the settings (instead of under) and under the weavings (instead of over).

☐ Pass this set of diagonals under the tips of the first diagonal on the top and bottom rails and over the tips of the diagonals on the side rails (fig. 8).

Plugging When both sets of diagonals have been completed, plugs of thin wood or cane are knocked into alternate holes, missing the corner holes and each hole adjacent to a corner. Knock the plugs in almost flush with the wood, and then to avoid damaging the chair work around the holes again with the clearer, knocking the plugs slightly below the level of the hole. The plugs should not project on the underside of the chair.

Turn the chair over and tidy up by cutting off all the ends flush against the wood, and cutting out long strands.

Beading Cut four pieces of No. 6 cane, each about 20·3 cm (8″) longer than the side of the chair seat. Damp and mellow them, and place 10·2 cm (4″) of the first piece down one corner with a temporary plug. Take a long strand of No. 1 or 2, pass it down through the unplugged hole next to the corner and secure it with a loop of cane underneath. Take the long length of cane over the length of No. 6 and pass it back down the same hole. Continue the lacing in each unplugged hole, being careful to maintain a good tension above and below.

This is made easier by lacing over a fat bodkin as well as the beading, and levering up the slack with the bodkin before extracting it. If the beading shows a tendency to rise at one edge or to veer away from the hole, bring the lacing down on that side and it will help to draw it back into place. At the next corner hole insert the beading but not the lacing strand, put in the next length of beading and before folding it down into place knock in a plug against the rough side of the cane, to give a neat corner.

Continue in the same way all round, crossing the lacing under the corner.

Curved frames

A dressing-table stool often has a dip in the middle of the frame at the front, and any such chair needs to be worked in a different sequence. The first setting must always be worked very tightly, from the centre of the dip to the sides. When doing the first weaving, take the strands *under* the setting, but not quite so tightly. The second setting goes under the first two stages, tightly again, and lying to the right of the first setting. From this point on, the weaving is finished off as usual.

You may be fortunate enough to have such a stool already, but if not, do remember to keep a look out in shops selling old furniture. You should also look out for chairs with broken seats.

Caning chair backs

There are a few points that are important to remember:

The smooth, shiny surface of the cane lies uppermost when being worked. It is more pliable if dampened and allowed to mellow before use.

Each chair must be carefully prepared. Always use the longest canes for the first stages.

A frame wider at the front than at the back

Most chairs tend to fall into this category, having more holes along the front rails than at the back.

First remove the seat. Turn the chair upside down, cut across all the strands between the holes, and carefully remove the old plugs. These should be put aside for replugging later.

First setting Lay the first setting strand down the middle of the frame working from the back to the front.

☐ Find centre hole in the back rail. Thread a long piece of cane down so that half its length is underneath the chair. Secure it firmly, shiny side uppermost, either with a peg, or by looping the lower end through the frame and down the same hole under the top end. When the cane is put under tension, the long length bites on the loop and prevents it from slipping.

☐ Lay settings until all the holes along the back rail are filled, except for the corners.

Because there are more holes in the front rail, there will be several empty holes on each side.

Fill these by working parallel settings taken to appropriate holes on the sides.

☐ Complete these strands until only the corners are left empty.

First weaving The first weaving takes the strands across the frame from side to side.

☐ Take the end of a cane piece across the underside of the corner and come up through the first hole on the side rail next to the empty corner hole.

☐ Lay strand over the first settings to the corresponding hole on the opposite rail. Repeat, working from side to side until all the holes are used up apart from the corners.

☐ When first setting and first weaving are complete, the pattern should look as in fig. 1.

Second setting and weaving Follow the usual sequence for setting and weaving, laying the second setting

to the left of the first and weave the second weaving to the back of the first.

Diagonals are worked in a slightly different way to those described for the square chair.

Imagine a rectangular side rising from the bottom left corner. As the diagonals reach it approaching from a south easterly direction, they find that the top corner has been cut off so there are some holes missing. The diagonals are forced to converge at this point. The convergences are called 'doubles'.

Again, imagine a rectangular side dropping down from the top right corner. The diagonals are pointing towards it from a north westerly direction. As they approach it is obvious that there are extra settings to be dealt with. There are too many holes in this case so some will have to be left empty. These are called 'misses'.

These two principles apply to any irregularly shaped frame, and though it may sound difficult, once the basic idea has been grasped, it is easy to apply.

When taking the first diagonal over a weaving tip on the side rails, the following should happen automatically.

☐ The 'doubles' (or 'misses') will be in 1st or 2nd hole below the top of a short setting.

☐ The strands curve slightly, but the higher the 'double' (or 'miss') occurs the better, for it will cover the wood with a closer, more even texture of canework.

☐ When weaving diagonals to their fullest extent (this means always using the tips first and last), 'doubles' and 'misses' will automatically occur at the best place. If in doubt about the pattern that is forming, leave the end of the diagonal row or rows free, with several inches of cane to spare.

☐ Continue weaving and when the

1. First setting and weaving on a frame wider at the front than at the back.
2. Beginning the first diagonal crossing. X marks any 'doubles', and O 'misses'.
3. First setting and weaving on a bow fronted frame.

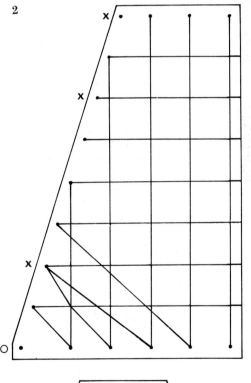

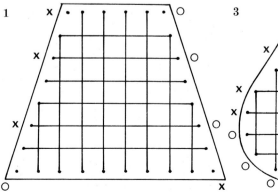

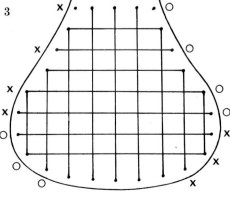

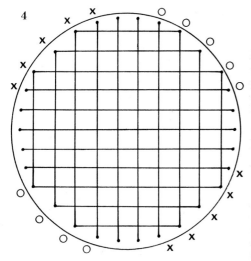

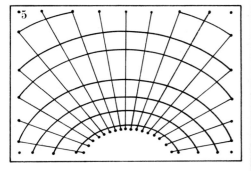

4. *First setting and weaving on a circular shaped frame.*
5. *First setting and weaving for a rising sun design.*

pattern is clearly formed, go back and rearrange the doubtful ends.

☐ Next work second set of diagonals. These will 'miss' in the holes that were doubled, and 'double' in the holes that were missed the first time, such as in the corners.

Fig. 2 shows the beginning of a first crossing. The places to 'double' are marked X and the 'misses' are marked 0.

A bow fronted frame

Put in the settings in the usual way. Stop when the distance between the last setting and the hole furthest away on that same side, is about the average distance between the settings.

☐ Start first weaving from the back, making sure that the line of the first weaving is straight.

☐ Take the bottom of shortest settings as the corners. Any short weaving between them will require 'doubles' and 'misses'.

☐ Start crossings in the middle of the front of the seat. Start and finish by using a tip as usual.

☐ Fig. 3 illustrates completed setting and weaving.

☐ Work second setting and weaving in the manner previously described.

☐ Finally place diagonals following the basic principles explained for the first chair.

A circular frame

It is vital on a circular frame to place the first line of setting correctly.

☐ Find hole that lies in the centre back of the chair frame. Count the holes to either side of this hole to find the centre of the sides.

☐ To keep settings parallel and evenly spaced, it will be necessary to miss some of the holes towards the sides of the frame. See fig. 4.

☐ Find centre holes at the sides to start weaving, spacing the strands in the same way as for the settings.

☐ Start crossings in the middle of the front of the frame.

On the first crossing there will be a group of 'doubles' in the top left and bottom right areas, and a group of 'misses' in the bottom left and top right areas. Take the holes between the shortest settings and the shortest weavings to represent the corners.

A frame with a 'Rising Sun' design

These last two shapes, the Rising Sun and the Spider's Web, are for advanced practitioners only. They should only be attempted after a lot of practice on the basic shapes.

A Rising Sun chairback has a semi-circular block of wood on the top or bottom rail bearing a number of very finely drilled holes. The number of these holes usually corresponds with the total number of holes on the other three sides. It is advisable to keep the old piece of caning for reference, so remove it carefully and lay it on one side before you start.

The rising sun pattern is formed by laying the settings from the semi-circular block to the corresponding holes on the other three sides of the frame. The effect is similar to the rays of the sun, hence the name of the design.

If there are extra holes, simply space the rays evenly and leave them empty.

☐ First lay both settings. Then work two weavings, starting next to the block and curving them in the same way.

☐ Work both weavings between same holes before moving on to the next pair.

☐ If 'sun' is in a square or rectangular shape, there will probably be some extra short weavings across the corners. As usual, the first diagonals go under the settings and over the weavings.

☐ The holes in the sun are plugged with match sticks or glued.

Spider's Web

This type of chair has a central block completely detached from the outer frame. It is held in the centre of the frame by the canework, and therefore floats freely when the chair is cleared for re-caning.

☐ Position block in the centre of the frame and hold it in place temporarily with thin wire, fishing line or odd lengths of cane.

☐ Thread one of these materials from top centre of the frame, through the top and bottom holes of the centre block, to the bottom of the frame.

☐ Put a similar line across frame using the same technique, and slide the block into the correct position.

The settings radiate from the block to the sides of the frame.

☐ Start in two places opposite each other so as not to pull the block out of place, and work at them alternately.

☐ Work the pairs of settings firmly once the correct position of the block has been established.

☐ Work the weavers in pairs.

These will spiral round from the centre block, moving out to a distance of about 2·5 cm (1″), and continuing until the outside frame is reached.

When it is necessary to make a join, overlap the ends to be cut off at a later stage and finally add a touch of glue to keep them firm.

When all the crossings are in position, adjust the tension as necessary. ·

The holes in the centre block must always be plugged.

Beading on curved shapes It is very important that the beading cane should lie flat before it is laced.

For a bow fronted frame, cut a piece of cane long enough to go down both sides and round the front of the frame.

For a circular frame, cut a piece of cane long enough to go all the way round the frame.

☐ Damp and mellow beading. When it is sufficiently pliable, hold it onto the frame firmly with three fingers of the left hand. Pull it round into shape with the right hand with a quick succession of movements, while following with the left hand to press and flatten the curve. It should lie smoothly in place after moulding.

If beading a bow fronted chair, one plug can be left out on the sharpest curve and an extra lacing stitch worked.

On a circular chair, leave the centre back hole unplugged, the two holes on each side and alternate holes thereafter.

The beginning and end of the beading are completed by inserting the ends down the centre back hole where they can be plugged and tidied up on the underside of the chair.

Raffia basket

Raffia work, in the pleasing natural material, can be used to make any number of attractive and useful items, from tablemats to baskets. There are several different ways of using raffia; it makes a brilliant embroidery thread; it can be wound and woven over a cardboard base, it can be woven to produce a piece of fabric. It can also be coiled and twisted around thick sisal string to make a really firm structure, such as the beach basket shown here. Raffia work is a fascinating craft—and it's ideal to take away for something to do on holiday—light, easy to carry, and very relaxing once you've mastered the basic techniques of this traditional craft.

Tools

A needle with a large eye and a blunt point (a No. 14 tapestry needle is ideal) and a pair of scissors are all the tools needed for raffia work.

Methods of working. Begin by working a coil for the foundation row.

☐ Cut sisal string diagonally 2·5 cm (1″) making a kind of point to reduce

This attractive raffia beach basket is both useful and decorative. It is woven in a pretty openwork design.

thickness in the finished join when the end is tucked in. Run string through beeswax, to reduce the number of hairs that stand up. Thread needle with enough strands of raffia to equal the thickness of one ply of the sisal string.

☐ Using left forefinger and thumb, hold both the cut end of sisal string and one end of the raffia, leaving the other end of raffia, with the needle attached, hanging free (diagram 1).

☐ With right forefinger and thumb, hold only the raffia, still leaving needle hanging free. The raffia, now held with the right forefinger and thumb, is in position to coil on to the sisal string to make the foundation row (referred to from now on as 'the row below') (diagram 2).

To do this, proceed as follows:

☐ Using right forefinger and thumb, twist the raffia evenly for 2·5cm (1″) then coil that twisted raffia, working away from you, around the sisal string, as if you were turning the handle of a sewing machine. Thus you will get a good, even tension. Twist another unit of raffia and coil that around, keeping the raffia taut all the time to stop it unwinding. Continue covering the sisal string with twisted raffia, bending the string to form a circle.

To join tuck the end of the sisal into the first one or two coils and resume coiling until the whole ring is completely covered (diagram 3).

The foundation row or the 'row below' is now completely covered with twisted raffia. Continue to cover the sisal string with the twisted raffia for six or eight coils; this is the beginning of your second circle. You can continue to work in circles, to make a tablemat, as shown in diagrams 4 and 5, in which single and double stitches are used.

Single stitch. To make a single stitch for connecting your second row to your first row, still twisting the raffia, take it into the row below, bring it up to the other side and over the row you have started to work. The needle now comes into use for uniting the two shanks of raffia.

☐ Take raffia (not twisted) and the needle around the two shanks, from left to right, pulling shanks tightly together so they meet. Meanwhile, with the left forefinger and thumb, hold the row you are working and the row below, so that a flat shape is achieved. Go round the shanks twice more with untwisted raffia. Be sure always to come out on the left-hand side, so the work will look the same on both sides.

Double Stitch. This is made by forming shanks, as for the single stitch, one on either side of the stitch in the row below, and then united by untwisted raffia.

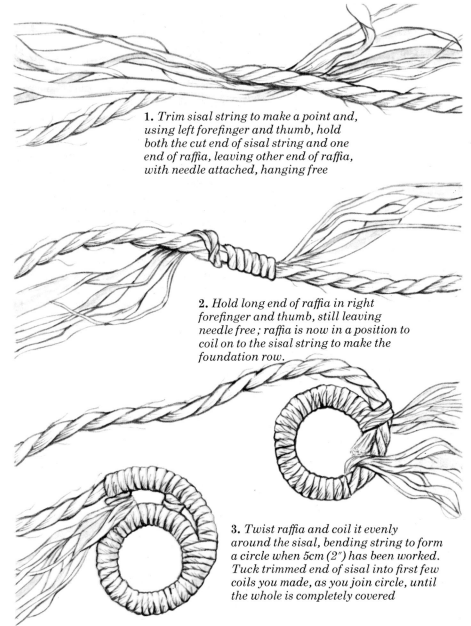

1. *Trim sisal string to make a point and, using left forefinger and thumb, hold both the cut end of sisal string and one end of raffia, leaving other end of raffia, with needle attached, hanging free*

2. *Hold long end of raffia in right forefinger and thumb, still leaving needle free; raffia is now in a position to coil on to the sisal string to make the foundation row.*

3. *Twist raffia and coil it evenly around the sisal, bending string to form a circle when 5cm (2″) has been worked. Tuck trimmed end of sisal into first few coils you made, as you join circle, until the whole is completely covered*

4. *To start a second circle, cover the sisal with twisted raffia for six or eight coils, then work a single stitch; to do this, still twisting the raffia, take it under the row below, bring it up the other side and the row you are working on then, using needle and untwisted raffia, go around the two shanks three times, from left to right, pulling shanks together and coming out on the left.*

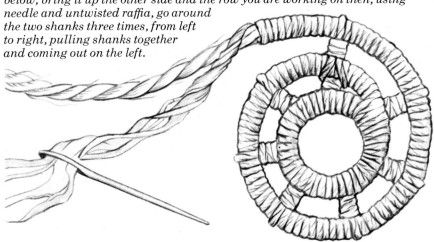

5. *Start a third circle, then work a double stitch; to do this, work shanks— as described in diagram 4—one on either side of the stitch in the row below, and unite them with untwisted raffia.*

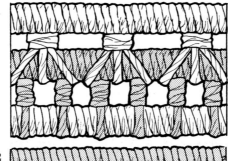

1. *The single stitch described in the text is shown on the lower row of this detail, with single stitches worked on the row below.*

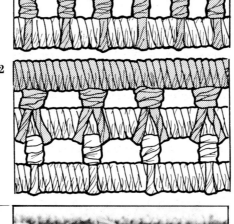

2. *The double stitch described in the text is shown on the top row of this detail, with single stitches worked on the row below.*

For the basket sides

1st row: Work single stitches into the fillis string, working 7 stitches to every 7.5cm (3").

2nd row: Work one double stitch into each single stitch in row below

3rd row: Work one treble stitch into each two double stitches below

4th row: Work single stitches into row below, two stitches over each treble

5th row: Work in single stitch, one stitch to either side of two single stitches in row below

6th row: Work two single stitches inside every two stitches in row below

7th row: Work one single stitch between each two in row below

8th row: Work one single stitch either side of single stitches in row below

9th row: Work two single stitches between groups of two stitches in row below

10th row: Work single stitches in groups of two between groups of two in row below

11th row: Work one single stitch into centre of each two in row below

12th row: Work three single stitches between each stitch in row below

13th row: Work one treble stitch over every two stitches in row below

14th row: Work one treble over every two treble stitches in row below

15th row: Work one single stitch either side of each treble in row below

16th row: Work one treble over each two singles in row below, and one single between each treble

17th row: Work two trebles over every three trebles in row below

18th row: Work two singles between each treble of row below

19th row: Work one double stitch over two single stitches in row below, leaving one single stitch free between each double

Now work handles

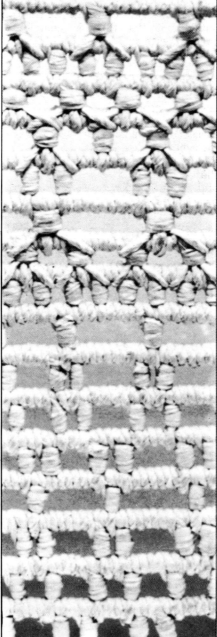

Treble Stitch. To form a treble stitch, the row below must have two stitches close together. Make the shanks of the first stitch to the right of the two stitches below; make the second between the two stitches, and the third on the left of the two stitches. Unite these three shanks as the double stitch, using untwisted raffia.

When you have mastered these basic stitches, you will be able to design your own work, or make our beach basket.

Beach basket

You will need

0.45g (1lb) natural, dry raffia
Sisal string
Beeswax
One hank of fillis or soft white garden string
2 No. 12 or 14 tapestry needles
Scissors
A plywood basket base, ready bored, available in different shapes and sizes

To prepare the basket base Using fillis string and the two tapestry needles, thread string both ways through each hole on plywood base, threading needles and string opposite ways through one hole and working all the way around, so both sides of plywood are completely threaded. Finish by tying a neat knot on the one side and work on this side, so the raffia work hides the knot.

Working the pattern. Follow the detail photograph of the basket's side for the pattern but, if you prefer, work out a random pattern of your own. Our basket measures approximately 21.5cm (9") deep by 49.5cm (19½") wide.

The handles

When the sides have been worked, mark out a space 17.8cm (7in) wide in the centre of the top row on both sides, using pieces of contrast thread.

☐ Work a row of single stitches into row below, working three single stitches to 2·5cm (1") starting from one left-hand piece of marker thread and working around to the opposite marker thread on the other side of basket.

☐ Wind twisted raffia around sisal for 29.2cm (11½") and then, leaving this length free for the handle, work single stitches into row below, exactly as before. When the marker thread on the opposite side is reached, wind twisted raffia around sisal for 29.2cm (11½") and then work a row of treble stitch, making 3 treble stitches to every 5cm (2") all around basket, working each treble stitch over two shanks of the row below. When the prepared handle sections are reached, work single stitches. Work a final row, working single stitches between double stitches: 3 double stitches and 2 single stitches to 2.5cm (1in). Work treble stitches over handles.

Corn dollies

Corn Dollies are part of ancient harvest ritual. The Dolly, or idol as in the group shown in the picture, was a symbol of fertility which farmers were anxious to preserve from one harvest to the next. A Dolly was usually made with straw from the last sheaf. Mechanisation has meant that straw is now grown much shorter than it used to be, but since the revival of interest in the craft, long and hollow stemmed varieties of straw are sometimes grown specially to make Dollies.

Learn the techniques of this fascinating country craft by making an appealing straw angel. As you follow the pattern, you will be learning some very useful techniques. These can be adapted to making other Dollies, such as those shown in the illustration overleaf.

Materials required to make the angel

measuring 23cm (9″) high:
bundle of oat straws, or Art Straws
bundle of rye straws, or Art Straws
sheet of stiff card 18cm by 7.5cm
(7″ by 3″)
glue
damp cloth or towel
strong linen or cotton thread
scissors
small sharp knife

Preparing the straw Oat and rye straws are specified in the instructions, but wheat straw, which is more easily obtainable, can be substituted. The straw must be specially prepared, or 'tempered', so that it becomes pliable and easy to work. It should be damp enough to bend easily without splitting, but not soggy.

☐ Cut the straw above first joint and below the ear as shown in the diagram.

☐ Put cut straw into enough water to cover it completely then leave it to soak for 10 minutes. Wrap the straw in a damp towel or cloth and leave it for 2 to 3 hours.

☐ While you are working, keep the straw not actually in use wrapped in the damp cloth to prevent it drying out. Any straw that is left over from a single project should be dried completely in warm air or in a cool oven. It can then be stored in a dry place and tempered again when you wish to use it.

Joining the straw A single straw may often be too short to complete some of the plaits. If so, join two straws by inserting a slant-cut tip into a straight-cut end as shown in the diagram. The join should be made under a fold in the plait where it cannot be seen.

To make the angel

The body: Roll the card into a cylinder 18cm (7″) long and 2cm (¾″) across. Glue into position.

☐ Take enough of prepared oat straws to completely cover the outside of the tube, making sure to have an odd number. Cut them into 23cm (9″) lengths and carefully slit them down one side. Open the straws out flat.

☐ Take each straw in turn, glue 2.5cm (1″) of the dull side of the straw inside one end of the tube. Bend the rest of the straw over the edge as shown in the diagram, and press closely against the cardboard. Continue until the outside of the tube is completely covered, with an odd number of straws.

☐ Take a narrow straw, as long as possible, slit it open and weave it round the tube, over one straw and under the next, until the tube is completely enclosed.

When the weaving is complete, tuck the ends of the 23cm (9″) strips inside the tube and glue down.

The head: This is formed from a Four Plait 12.5cm (5″) long. To work the plait, take 4 straws and, working on a firm flat surface, lay them out as shown in the diagram. Take straw A over C to lie beside B. Then bring B down over D into the space left by A. Turn the work a quarter circle clockwise. Repeat the two part manoeuvre and turn again. Continue in this way until the plait is the required length. Always fold the plaits closely to make a sharp concertina-like edge. Join the ends of the plait and glue them just inside the top of the cylinder.

The halo: Make a Six Plait 18cm (7″) long. Take 6 of the longest oat straws and lay them out as shown in the diagram. Fold B over to lie between A and F; then take A over to lie between C and E; E crosses to lie between D and B; B crosses to lie between A and F; F crosses to lie between E and C; C crosses to lie between B and D. Continue, folding D, A, E, B, F and C until the plait is the required length. Fix the halo to the outside of the cylinder behind the head. If you find it difficult to understand this plait, practise first with labelled strips of paper.

The arms: These are formed from a 23cm (9″) long Zwemmer Plait. Following the diagrams, take two long oat straws and cross CD over the centre of BA. Then take A over D to lie alongside C (Fig. 1).

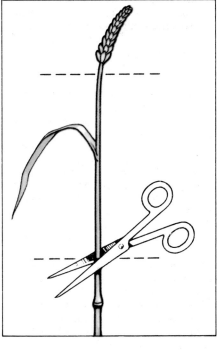

Top: a close-up detail of the corn dolly described in this pattern, with demurely folded arms and pretty angel wings formed from straws.

Above: cutting the straw.

Take B under C and over A to lie alongside D (Fig. 2) Take C under A and B and over D (Fig. 3). Take C under D and over B to lie alongside A (Fig. 4). Take D under B and C and over A (Fig. 5).

The straws will now form the same shape as in Fig. 2. Continue with the plait, working stages 2, 3, 4 and 5 as shown in the diagrams until it is the required length.

Lay the arm plait across the top of the cylinder in front of the head and stitch or glue into position.

The wings: Take a bundle of rye straws, 46cm (18″) long. Tie them tightly in the centre so that they fan out around one central straight straw. Hold them in position with a row of pairing 5cm (2″) on either side of the centre. To work pairing, follow the diagram. Fold all the straws on a line running from 9cm to 6·5cm (3½″ to 2½″) away from the centre. Pair across the bottom of the wing, about 11·5cm (4½″) from the top fold and then trim the ends to a point.

If you have trouble getting the wings to stay in position, re-damp them and put them upside down in a container of suitable size. Let them dry in the right position. Pin the wings to the body, beneath the halo.

Be sure to dry the angel thoroughly, under the plaits and in the folds, before putting it away. Keep it in a dry place.

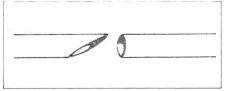

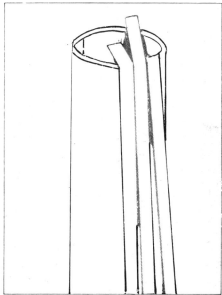

Top: joining two straws.

Below: gluing straws over the tube.

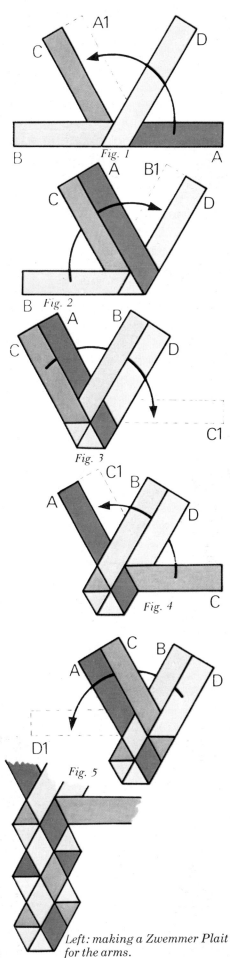

Left: making a Zwemmer Plait for the arms.

63

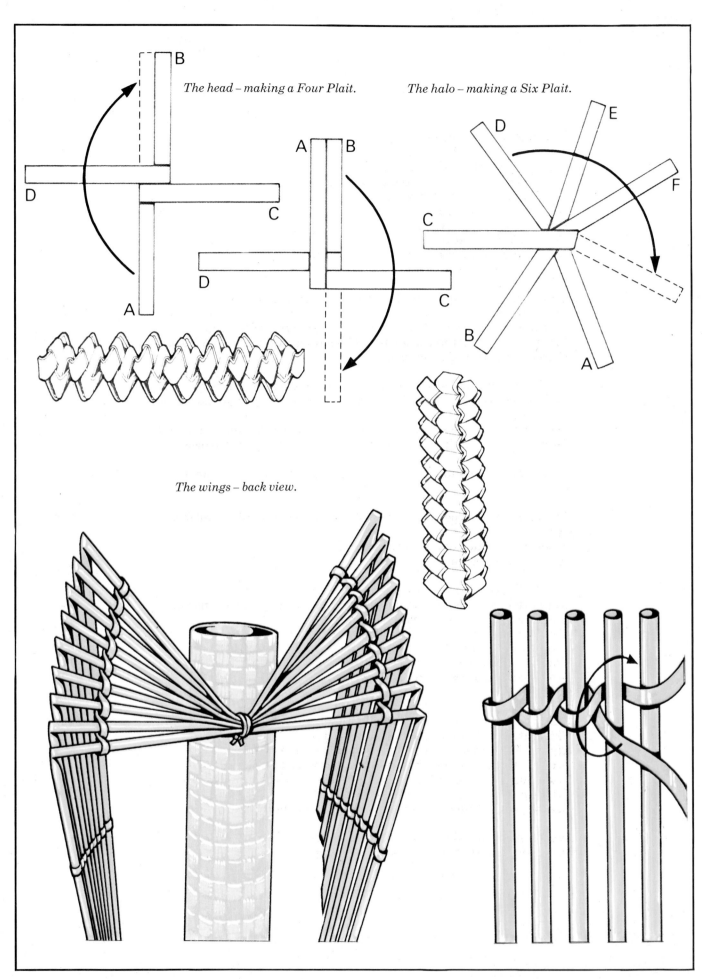

The head – making a Four Plait.

The halo – making a Six Plait.

The wings – back view.